# Successful
# Lifelong Learning

## *Ten Tactics for Today and Tomorrow*
### Revised Edition

## Robert L. Steinbach

## *A Fifty-Minute™ Series Book*

# Successful Lifelong Learning

*Ten Tactics for Today and Tomorrow*

Revised Edition (formerly *The Adult Learner*)

**Robert L. Steinbach**

**CREDITS:**
Senior Editor: **Debbie Woodbury**
Production Manager: **Judy Petry**
Cover: **Amy Shayne and Fifth Street Design**
Copy Editor: **Charlotte Bosarge**
Artwork: **Ralph Mapson and L. Kelly Lyles**
Text Design: **Amy Shayne**
Production Artist: **Robin Strobel**

© 1990, 2000 Crisp Publications, Inc.
Printed in the United States of America by Von Hoffmann Graphics, Inc.

CrispLearning.com

02   10 9 8 7 6 5

Library of Congress Catalog Card Number 99-70551
Steinbach, Robert L.
Successful Lifelong Learning, Revised Edition
Ten Tactics for Today and Tomorrow
ISBN 1-56052-563-0

This book is printed on recyclable paper with soy ink.

# Learning Objectives For:

## SUCCESSFUL LIFELONG LEARNING

The objectives for *Successful Lifelong Learning* are listed below.
They have been developed to guide you, the reader, to the core issues
covered in this book.

### THE OBJECTIVES OF THIS BOOK ARE:

❑ 1) To demonstrate why continual learning is a vital part of
modern life

❑ 2) To help readers understand and capitalize on their unique
learning style

❑ 3) To explain techniques for improving listening, concentration,
memory, and reading comprehension

❑ 4) To illustrate the role that technology, habits, and experience can
play in sucessful learning

❑ 5) To present information about various lifelong learning options and
to encourage readers to begin planning for their own learning in a
proactive, purposeful way

### ASSESSING YOUR PROGRESS

In addition to the learning objectives, Crisp Learning has developed an
**assessment** that covers the fundamental information presented in this
book. A 25-item, multiple-choice and true-false questionnaire allows the
reader to evaluate his or her comprehension of the subject matter. To learn
how to obtain a copy of this assessment, please call **1-800-442-7477** and
ask to speak with a Customer Service Representative.

*Assessments should not be used in any employee selection process.*

# About the Author

Bob Steinbach is the founder and President of Skill Development Consultants (SDC), an international performance consulting company. Since 1983, SDC has provided training, facilitation, and consulting services to a variety of organizations, including: General Motors, the City of Dayton, Louisville Gas and Electric, IBM, Subaru-Isuzu America, Schumberger ATE, and Saturn Corporation.

In 1998, SDC was selected to design and deliver training in coaching skills for the managers and peer coaches of Schlumberger ATE, a high-tech, multi-national corporation. In one three-month period, Bob conducted over 30 highly-evaluated workshops in North America, Europe, and Asia.

SDC provides customized performance improvement interventions that include needs assessments, skill analysis, training programs, and meeting and retreat facilitation. In addition, Mr. Steinbach speaks to conferences and professional groups on a variety of topics related to improving individual and group performance. He earned both his Bachelor of Science and Master of Education degrees from Bowling Green State University in Bowling Green, Ohio.

**For information about workshops and presentations based on this book, contact:**

**Skill Development Consultants**

**Dayton, Ohio**

**937-426-6776**

**steinb@aol.com**

# Contents

## Section I: Lifelong Learning and You

## Section II: Improving Listening, Memory, and Reading Skills

## Section III: Making Technology, Habits, and Experience Work for You

# SECTION 1

# Lifelong Learning and You

2

# Introduction: Why Lifelong Learning?

"What will I learn today?" That may be the most important question you can ask yourself as you start each day. What you learn today and in the future could very well determine the course and quality of the rest of your life.

Learning increases the number of choices available to you; acting on those choices can drastically improve the quality of your life. In a very real sense you are what you learn and choose to put into practice.

## *Why bother?*

This book is about self-directed, lifelong learning; why it is essential to your future, and how to do it effectively. Let's start with the *why* of lifelong learning; because if you are not convinced that being a self-directed, successful lifelong learner is in your best interest, no amount of how-to tips will do any good. Here are just a few reasons for making lifelong learning a personal goal.

### REASON 1: Today's Rapid Pace of Change

We are experiencing greater change at a more rapid pace than in any period of human history, and, odds are, it will only speed up. According to the U.S. Patent and Trademark Office, twice as many patents were granted in 1998 as in 1980. Many of those newly patented products will find their way into your home or workplace. The people who learn to use those new gadgets will have an advantage. And the quicker they learn, the greater their advantage will be.

Remember when only a few people had cell phones? When only technology buffs had home computers? Think about the people that embraced the computer early on; think of the advantage that they had as computers began to spring up everywhere. Some of those people became millionaires (or billionaires), others just got excellent jobs, and yes, some even got laid off from those jobs. But even those people who lost a job in the shake-ups of the last couple of decades had a tremendous advantage; they had learned a skill that was extremely valuable. That put them in a much better position to re-enter the workforce on their own terms.

## REASON 2: Economic Opportunity

The world needs people with many different ambitions and skills. No matter what your interests, or what your field, if you know something valuable and you are willing and able to learn more, you have an economic advantage in a rapidly changing world. That's one reason that becoming an aggressive and effective lifelong learner is in your best interest. You will have more choices about how you make a living, and you will be in more demand to employers in the "knowledge economy."

## REASON 3: Quality of Life

Beyond economics, learning for its own sake can enrich your life, at any age. People are living longer, but are we living better? One way to improve the quality of your life is to look for those opportunities to make every day a chance for personal growth and enrichment. Early in life, learning for the sake of learning often takes a back seat to required courses, job-related training, and other things we "have to do." One of the joys of self-directed learning is the decision to learn what you want, when you want. If you get in the habit of learning for the fun of it, life will become more interesting and so will you.

## REASON 4: Security

The people who feel secure in this constantly changing world will be those who are confident that they can learn new skills. The kind of security based solely on loyalty and seniority is largely gone. The kind of security based on your current knowledge and skills is better, as long as those skills stay in demand. The kind of security based on your ability to learn new skills throughout your lifetime is your best bet. Neglecting to learn new skills makes you vulnerable to unexpected changes in both personal and professional life. Waiting until those changes occur before broadening your skills can be a risky tactic.

## REASON 5: Human Nature

Humans are designed to learn from the moment of birth; learning should be a lifelong process. Great minds in history like Leonardo da Vinci, Abraham Lincoln, Helen Keller, and Malcolm X were all lifelong learners who sought opportunities to master new skills, meet new challenges, and gain new knowledge throughout their lives.

Being a lifelong learner is a competitive advantage, adds to your quality of life, and can be a matter of economic survival. In this book, you will explore how to find and take advantage of the learning opportunities that are all around you. You will learn skills that can enable you to make the most of training, on-the-job learning, and formal schooling.

It's easy to yearn for the good old days when you could "hang in there" and let your seniority protect you until retirement. It's easy to resent technological advances, instability in the job market, and the other forces that make learning essential to a successful life. It's easy to think that other people are forcing you into a kind of perpetual improvement process.

However, you shouldn't think you are learning for somebody else. Even though your company may require training, the time and effort you spend on learning is an investment in yourself and your future. Not only should you learn when you must learn, you need to seek out the opportunity. The future belongs to those who can best keep up with the changes around them.

## A Bonus:

Stretching yourself intellectually will help keep you mentally younger. The old adage "use it or lose it" applies to mental as well as physical well-being. Lifelong learners are sharper, more interesting, and more alive.

The opportunity to learn and to grow is all around you. It's in your job, in your community, through the Internet, and in self-study books like the one you are now reading. You will find opportunities to learn every day, *if you are looking for them*. Looking for, and taking advantage of, those daily opportunities can make a drastic difference in how you spend the rest of your life. Learning shouldn't be a chore—it should be an adventure.

Look around you today; what opportunities are there for you to explore new kinds of knowledge and acquire new skills? What challenges can you take on at work that will stretch you? What new book, website, audiotape, or conversation could expand how you view yourself and your world? The quote below sums up the *why* of lifelong learning pretty well.

> **"** *In times of change, learners inherit the earth, while the learned find themselves beautifully equipped to deal with a world that no longer exists."*
>
> —Eric Hoffer

6

## RON: A CASE STUDY

Ron has worked for the same large company for 24 years. At age 48, he has a family, house, two cars, and a boat. He hopes to retire in his mid 50's and enjoy the company's retirement benefits and health plan. In the last few years, however, the company has been shaken by stiff competition and a dependence on outdated technology. Recently, there has been talk of a merger and Ron isn't sure what that will mean for his future. Many of his coworkers have adopted a wait-and-see attitude and spend their time talking about early retirement and buy-outs.

Ron's company has been trying to break into new markets with different technology. Ron feels intimidated by new high-tech alternatives. The company is requiring training in some areas, like teamwork and communication skills. There are also opportunities to learn the new technologies both on the job and through classes.

Many employees Ron's age see this training as a waste of time. Ron would rather keep doing what he is good at, rather than sit in a classroom.

Why should Ron bother with "school" at this stage of his life?

## YOUR ADVICE TO RON

Pretend you are a close friend or relative of Ron and then answer the questions below.

**What would you tell Ron about planning for his future?** _____

_____

_____

**What would you say about the training opportunities that are being offered to him?** _____

_____

_____

**Do you have anything in common with Ron? If so, what?** _____

_____

_____

## THE AUTHOR'S ADVICE TO RON

Tens of thousands of American workers can identify with Ron's situation. Many people who believed they had very stable jobs are now worried.

Ron should get involved in training programs offered by his company. The only way for companies to maintain a leadership position in a changing economy is to invest heavily in employee education and training. The old way of working is too expensive and slow to be competitive in the digital world. Being an expert in outdated technology has little value. Individuals and organizations must be able to compete with skills and knowledge that will be in demand in the future.

**There are at least three reasons for Ron to upgrade his skills:**

➤ **First:** to benefit the company by becoming a more valuable employee. Remember those retirement benefits Ron is counting on? Healthy companies can afford to pay healthy benefits, sick ones can't.

➤ **Second:** to protect himself. Whatever he learns makes him more valuable. If Ron is ever out of work, knowing about digital technology or self-directed teams might make the difference between his getting a good job or flipping burgers.

➤ **Third:** Ron mentioned retiring in his mid 50's. If he lives to an average life expectancy, he will be around at least 20+ years after retirement. Many people who retire at a fairly young age take another job or start their own business. Long retirements can be both expensive and boring. Whatever he learns now will help him enrich the rest of his life.

## THE AUTHOR'S ADVICE TO THE READER

If you are pinning your hopes on finding (or keeping) a lifetime job in a large corporation, good luck. Ron's long career with one company was typical in the 1950s, '60s, and '70s, but is now very rare. Experts predict today's new workers will change jobs five to ten times in their lifetime. Most job growth potential lies with small companies; large companies continue to try to reduce staff. Job security in the next century will come from what you know and what you can learn, not your seniority date.

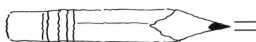

# EXERCISE: WHAT'S IN IT FOR ME?

The motivation to be a lifelong learner is different for each person. Check (✓) all the reasons that you believe being a lifelong learner is important to you, personally. Then, circle the five that are of particular importance to you at this stage of your life:

\_\_\_\_\_ **Learning increases the number of job options that I will have**

\_\_\_\_\_ **Learning increases the number of options I will have in my personal life**

\_\_\_\_\_ **Learning will make me more valuable to my current employer**

\_\_\_\_\_ **Learning will make me more valuable to future employers**

\_\_\_\_\_ **Learning is enjoyable, for its own sake**

\_\_\_\_\_ **Learning will help me adapt to changes in my personal life**

\_\_\_\_\_ **Learning will make my life more interesting and enjoyable**

\_\_\_\_\_ **Learning puts me more in control of my future**

\_\_\_\_\_ **Learning will help me do my current job better**

\_\_\_\_\_ **Learning will help keep me mentally young**

\_\_\_\_\_ **Learning makes me a more interesting person**

\_\_\_\_\_ **Learning makes me a more interested person**

\_\_\_\_\_ **Learning will help me be a better provider**

\_\_\_\_\_ **Learning will help me set a good example for my family or friends**

\_\_\_\_\_ **Learning will help me improve my life financially**

\_\_\_\_\_ **Learning will help me adapt to changes in my professional life**

\_\_\_\_\_ **Learning will increase the meaning in my life**

Note: All of these are great reasons to be a lifelong learner. As you read this book, and as you pursue other learning opportunities, keep in mind those reasons that are the most meaningful and relevant to you.

# Tactic 1: Planning for Lifelong Learning

So what do you want to learn? That is a very important question to answer. We are truly in an era of information overload. The sheer amount of learning options can lead us to get in over our heads; trying to skip to the "good stuff" without mastering the basics. Where should you start? Answering the questions below is a first step.

## Why you are interested in additional learning right now?

To get a better job? To expand your career options? To get more control over your personal life? To learn for the sake of learning?

## What skill or knowledge do you need to acquire?

What do you need to know to meet your goals? Avoid thinking in terms of "degrees" or even courses right now; think only about the content.

## How can you best meet your learning needs?

How do you best learn? You will learn more about your learning preferences after you complete the activities in Tactic 3. Do you have time to go to formal classes? If not, what other options are available?

## Where do you need to start?

What is your current skill level? Do you need to master the basics before moving on to what really interests you? Don't start with Calculus if you never quite "got" Algebra.

## How much do you need to know?

Do you need a degree in Computer Graphics or do you need to learn how to deliver a really good presentation? Do you need a degree in Communications or do you simply need to learn to be more assertive?

# *Are you willing to make learning a priority?*

Many people find that they are filled with good intentions about being a lifelong learner, but they never seem to get around to it. Interesting ideas and opportunities cross their path, but they always seem to be too late for registration, or they can't find the time to use the self-study cassettes they ordered. If learning is to be a priority, you must treat it like one. The following steps will help you get started.

## 1 Set some learning goals.

Think about those things that you would like to know more about or be better at. Write your goals down. Define what you want to learn by when.

## 2 Explore available resources.

Who teaches what you want to learn? What materials are within your reach? Self-study courses? Websites devoted to the topic? Many times these questions can be answered over the telephone or at the local library.

## 3 Include learning in your daily activities.

If you typically don't plan your day, now is a good time to start. Set aside 10 minutes in the morning or the evening before bed to think about what you would like to accomplish in the next day, including items related to your learning goals and self-improvement. Make a "to do" list that includes specific learning activities.

## 4 Decide when you will set aside time to learn on a regular basis.

The secret to successful learning is consistent effort. Practicing a skill 30 minutes a day, almost every day, is much more effective than cramming for several hours on the weekend now and then.

## 5 Take inventory of the materials and books that you already own.

Many of us are surrounded by unread books, cassettes we didn't listen to, half-started projects that we never took time to complete. You don't always have to spend more money to get started on lifelong learning. Often the materials you need are already on hand. A tremendous resource is the public library where books, magazines, tapes, and Internet access are available at no cost.

# 6 Set your goals high enough to challenge, but not so high that they frustrate you.

Tasks that are either too easy or too hard tend to discourage learners. To stay motivated, strive for goals that are possible but not pushovers.

# 7 Set "mini-goals" along the way.

If your goal is to be fluent in Spanish in five years, set a short-term goal of being able to order dinner at a Mexican restaurant in Spanish by the end of the month. Set an intermediate goal of being able to understand part of a Spanish language newscast by the end of the year. If you achieve your short-term goals, you will be on your way to achieving your long-term goal.

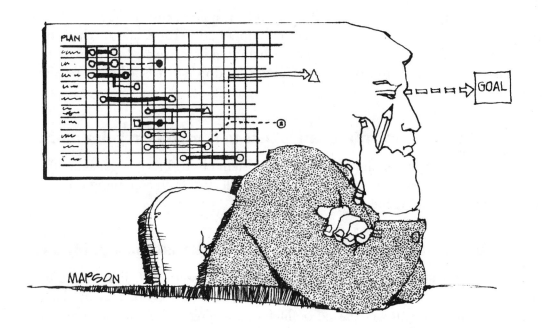

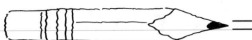

# EXERCISE: LEARNING GOALS WORK SHEET

Get specific about what you want to learn. Select one short-term (one month or less), one medium-term (one month to one year) and one long-term (longer than one year) learning goal. Start your learning journey by completing the form below. If you find it difficult to get specific now, mark this page, and come back when you are more certain about what you are interested in pursuing.

**Short-term learning goal:**

Within the next 30 days, I will learn: _____

Resources to meet this goal are available from: _____

I will set aside the following times to work toward this goal: _____

When I reach this goal, I will be able to: _____

**Medium-term learning goal:**

Within the next year, I will learn: _____

Resources to meet this goal are available from: _____

I will set aside the following times to work toward this goal: _____

When I reach this goal, I will be able to: _____

**Long-term learning goal:**

Within the next: _____ ,

I will learn: _____

Resources to meet this goal are available from: _____

I will set aside the following times to work toward this goal: _____

When I reach this goal, I will be able to: _____

# Tactic 2: Adopting the A.S.K. Attitude (Actively Seek Knowledge)

### Attitude Definition: _____

*manner, disposition ... tendency or orientation, especially of the mind.*

Children are aggressive learners who absorb information with or without teachers. In this book this approach to learning is called the A.S.K. (Actively Seek Knowledge) attitude.

Young children, especially before the age of five, are active learners. They are into everything: exploring, taking things apart, trying, succeeding, and failing. "Why?" is their favorite question. They don't wait for someone to motivate, reward, or even teach them. Children learn how to walk and how to speak a language with very little formal instruction. Children in a home where two languages are spoken learn both languages, naturally, without rules, studying, or tests. They learn without being self-conscious and without fear of failure.

Unfortunately, traditional schooling puts the learner in a passive role. Students become reactive and wait for the teacher to tell them what, when, and how to learn. Much of the joy of learning disappears during this process. Look in the window at a kindergarten class and watch the energy and movement; listen to the excited questions. Then check out a classroom full of adults. In most cases, they have been trained to wait silently for instructions. They worry about grades and stifle questions for fear of looking stupid.

Adults occasionally rediscover that childlike learner. When people discover a new hobby, most tear into it with pleasure. They read everything they can find on the subject, practice new techniques, and ask questions. They try and fail and try again. That kind of active learning is the key to successful lifelong learning.

# How do you start on the path of lifelong learning?

The truth is, you've already started. Unless you lock yourself in a room with no contact with the outside world, you will keep learning all your life whether you implement any of the ideas in this book or not. The question really is: how effective and consistent a learner are you? Do you seek out the learning opportunities around you and go forward in an enthusiastic, proactive manner? This book will accelerate and amplify your natural drive and ability to learn; it will help you make learning a conscious, intentional part of every day of your life.

## The Attitude of a Lifelong Learner

Being successful at lifelong learning starts with an attitude. Remember, to be an effective lifelong learner you should:

➤ **Look at each day as a learning opportunity ready to be exploited**

➤ **Know that expanding your skills at work is in your best interest, as well as your employer's**

➤ **View mistakes as opportunities to learn**

➤ **Understand that there are ways to think about everyday experiences that can increase your knowledge, insight, and skills**

---

## A.S.K.

**A**ctively **S**eek **K**nowledge

**A**lways **S**eek **K**nowledge

**A**ssertively **S**eek **K**nowledge

**A**ggressively **S**eek **K**nowledge

---

Get ready to put the A.S.K. attitude to work in this book, and in the rest of your life.

---

*(For more about the importance of attitude, see* <u>Attitude</u> *by Elwood N. Chapman, Crisp Publications, 1995.)*

# EXERCISE: TEXTBOOK PREVIEW

Before reading any further, explore the rest of this book. Read the Table of Contents. Skim through looking at headings, illustrations, and activities. When you see something interesting, stop and read a paragraph or two. Find at least six ideas/ concepts that you want to learn more about as you read the book. Record the concept and page number in the space below.

**PAGE NO.   IDEA**

_____   1. _____

_____   2. _____

_____   3. _____

_____   4. _____

_____   5. _____

_____   6. _____

Congratulations! You have just completed a textbook survey. This simple task has provided your brain with a road map and some destinations along this learning journey. You have readied yourself to learn by creating a partial image of the content of this book; your brain will naturally seek to complete this partial picture. A textbook survey helps prepare you to learn and motivates you to complete the task. You should always survey textbooks, manuals, and factual articles as a simple, effective way to increase reading comprehension and retention.

WARNING: If you did not complete the survey of the book or did not write down six things that you want to learn more about, you may be stuck in a passive, reactive learning mode.

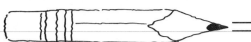

# EXERCISE: WHAT COULD YOU LEARN TODAY?

Make a special effort today to think about and look for opportunities to learn. What could you learn how to do, or learn more about, that would improve your life? Consider any kind of learning that would make you a better employee, business person, parent, or student. One guideline: be specific about what you want to learn. Don't make general statements about "finishing my degree." Think in terms of day-sized chunks. Use the space below to list five current areas of interest. Start your list now and add to it as the day goes on.

1. _____

_____

2. _____

_____

3. _____

_____

4. _____

_____

5. _____

_____

# Tactic 3:
# Learning about Your Learning Style

## Style Definition: _____

*a person's characteristic tastes, attitudes, and mode of behavior.*

## *You Have Style*

You have a style of dress, a style of speech, and a style of living. And you have a *learning* style. You can look around the room and get some idea of your living style, you can look in your closet to get an idea of your dress style, and you can look in your mirror to check out your hair style. But your learning style is a little different. You may not have given any thought to how you learn, and, especially, how you prefer to learn.

If you are going to be an effective lifelong learner, you'll need to get to know the way you function as a learner. The activities that follow will help you find out how you learn best and help you take control of your own learning. These activities will also help you to understand why some learning opportunities excite you while others put you to sleep. Most importantly, they will help you develop learning strategies that will make the best use of your individual learning style.

Complete each activity thoroughly, and then read the interpretation that follows. These activities are, by necessity, extremely brief. They are not thorough, scientific assessments and they will not give you the complete picture of your own learning style. But if you combine the results of the inventories with your own experience and self-assessment, you will gain valuable insights about yourself as a learner.

# EXERCISE: WHAT'S YOUR LEARNING STYLE?

Read each statement and then check *yes* or *no* depending on whether the statement describes, in general, how you learn. Be honest.

|  | YES | NO |
|---|---|---|
| I learn easily from listening to lectures, speeches, radio programs or audiotapes. | ____ | ____ |
| I usually figure out how to do new tasks by trial and error, with little help. | ____ | ____ |
| Books and other printed materials are easy for me to learn from. | ____ | ____ |
| Give me a map and I can usually find my way with little problem. | ____ | ____ |
| I need to have directions explained to me verbally to really understand. | ____ | ____ |
| I prefer to assemble something I've just purchased without looking at the instructions. | ____ | ____ |
| I learn a lot from discussions and debates. | ____ | ____ |
| I learn best if I have a new skill demonstrated for me before I try it. | ____ | ____ |
| The best way for me to learn how something works is to take it apart and put it back together. | ____ | ____ |
| I can remember most of what is said in classes and meetings without taking notes. | ____ | ____ |
| The classes that I was best at in school involved physical activity and movement. | ____ | ____ |
| Diagrams and drawings help me understand new concepts. | ____ | ____ |

# SELF-QUIZ RESULTS

While it is not an extensive scientific assessment, the self-quiz on the previous page can tell you something important about how you learn.

A "yes" to questions 1, 5, 7, and 10 indicates that you learn well by hearing: you are a "good listener" or strong *Auditory Learner*.

A "yes" to questions 3, 4, 8, and 12 indicates that you learn well by reading, watching and studying diagrams: you are a strong *Visual Learner*.

A "yes" to questions 2, 6, 9, and 11 indicates that you learn well by doing things, by using your body: you are a strong *Kinesthetic Learner*.

**Note:** It is very possible to have strong scores in more than one learning style.

Although a short quiz like this cannot diagnose how you learn with complete accuracy, it can provide insights into how you see yourself and the learning process. This is especially helpful in understanding how you match up with a particular learning task or instructor. Becoming a truly effective lifelong learner means maximizing your strengths and compensating for your limitations. By understanding your style, you can choose learning experiences that match your strengths, and adapt better to learning situations that challenge you.

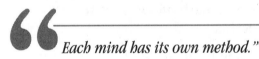

*Each mind has its own method."*

**—Ralph Waldo Emerson**

# What's Your Learning Style?

*Visual, auditory,* and *kinesthetic.* These words describe three of the main pathways new knowledge can follow on the way to your brain. Research shows that individuals tend to favor one or two of these styles over the others.

Children often exhibit preferences from a very early age. Some children show an early interest in colors and shapes, characteristic of a Visual Learner. Some children speak and understand language early, a characteristic of an Auditory Learner. Some children demonstrate an early ability to walk, throw a ball or put puzzles together, characteristic of a Kinesthetic Learner. These characteristics become a unique style of learning, each with its own strengths and weaknesses.

## *Visual Learners*

People who are primarily visual (sight-based) learners process the world best through their eyes. They notice how things look, they remember how a word is spelled by "seeing it" in their mind's eye. Visual learners love maps, charts, and diagrams, and they like to learn from reading books. They understand physical tasks better if someone shows them what to do. They like learning situations that include abundant visual aids.

Visual learners sometimes find lectures and discussions boring. Verbal directions often seem to "go in one ear and out the other." They can find it frustrating to be asked to do a task without a demonstration first. Since not all learning situations are designed specifically for visual learning, there are some adaptive strategies that visual learners can use.

### If you are a visual learner, try these strategies:

- ❏ **Read support material before a class lecture or meeting to prepare you to understand what is said.**

- ❏ **Ask for printed materials such as diagrams and charts.**

- ❏ **Use self-study videos and computer-assisted instruction that stimulate your visual sense.**

- ❏ **Ask this question when frustrated: "Will you *show* me. . ."**

- ❏ **Keep your learning space visually simple and filled only with items that support your learning.**

- ❏ **Take notes. Putting spoken words into print will help you recall what you heard.**

- ❏ **Draw diagrams of concepts that you are trying to learn; to you a picture really is worth a thousand words.**

# *Auditory Learners*

People who are primarily auditory (hearing-based) learners process the world best through their ears. They notice how things sound; they remember how a word is spelled by sounding it out in their "mind's ear." Auditory learners love lectures, discussions, radio news shows, and audiotapes, they like to learn from listening to, and interacting with, knowledgeable people. They tend to understand new tasks better if someone tells them what to do. They like learning situations that allow for asking and answering questions. Radio news and music can be important sources of stimulation for them.

Auditory learners sometimes find reading to be boring. Maps and written directions without a verbal explanation can be confusing. They may find it frustrating to be asked to do a task without a verbal explanation.

## If you are an auditory learner, try these strategies:

❑ **If possible, listen to a lecture or audiotape on a subject before reading new materials.**

❑ **Ask for a verbal explanation of printed materials such as diagrams and charts.**

❑ **Use self-study audiotapes and computer-assisted instruction with a sound track that will stimulate your auditory sense.**

❑ **Ask this question when frustrated: "Will you *explain to* me..."**

❑ **Use classical or light jazz music to shut out auditory distractions. Never try to listen to music with lyrics, radio news, or other meaningful auditory input while trying to read.**

❑ **Take notes. Capture main ideas to refer back to when studying.**

❑ **Find someone to discuss new concepts with. Talking and listening to them will help you integrate new ideas more easily.**

# Kinesthetic Learners

People who are primarily kinesthetic (movement-based) learners process the world best through their bodies. They respond to how things feel, remember the movements involved in a task, and they can remember how a word is spelled by writing it several times and remembering the "shape" of the word. Kinesthetic learners love labs, physical activity, and concrete learning aids that they can manipulate; they thrive on hands-on trial and error. They tend to understand better if they are able to try it themselves.

Kinesthetic learners sometimes find both reading and lectures boring. Verbal or written instructions without an opportunity to practice are often quickly forgotten. In the traditional classroom setting, they appear to have short attention spans, and, especially as children, tend to get in trouble for not being able to sit still. They can find it frustrating to be asked to be passive for a long period of time.

## If you are a kinesthetic learner, try these strategies:

❑ Seek learning situations and careers that allow for ample physical activity.

❑ Try drawing diagrams to illustrate abstract concepts.

❑ Construct a learning space that allows for active breaks; maybe even near exercise equipment.

❑ Ask this question when frustrated: "Will you let me *try* that. . ."

❑ Try standing up while you read or write (special tables are available for that purpose).

❑ Take notes. The physical act of writing will give you something to do as you listen and a record to refer to later.

# EXERCISE: A LEARNER'S AUTOBIOGRAPHY

An excellent way to understand your own learning style is to examine a successful learning experience from your past. Everyone has mastered some skill or body of knowledge that was challenging at first. If you think about your positive learning experiences, you may discover a personal pattern for successful learning.

The activity that follows will help you uncover how you learn best. You can use any body of knowledge or skill in which you excel. It can be work-related, hobby-related, something from your school days, knowledge of some part of popular culture—anything.

**First, pick your topic and then answer these questions:**

1. Describe a learning experience that you feel good about. It can be in or out of school, job- or hobby-related, recent or from many years ago.

   _____

   _____

2. What was your motivation for the learning?_____

   _____

3. Where did most of the learning take place? _____

   _____

4. How old were you at the time you started the learning? _____

5. How did you learn? What methods did you use to learn? _____

   _____

   _____

6. What were your feelings during the learning process? _____

   _____

7. How much time did you devote to the learning process? _____

   _____

8. Who helped you with your learning? How did he or she help?

   _____

# THINKING ABOUT YOUR LEARNER'S AUTOBIOGRAPHY

Most people can identify a pattern in their successful learning experiences. Look over your answers and try to determine yours. Do you work best alone or in a class? Are you primarily a visual, auditory, or kinesthetic learner, or do you utilize all three modes equally? What motivates you? What time of day and what type of learning location seem to help you do your best work?

You may also gain further information from thinking back on a failed learning project. Can you identify the cause of the failure? Was the project too difficult for your skill level? Did you fail to take an active role in your own learning? Were you reluctant to ask for help when you needed it? Was your motivation for the learning unclear? Did you talk yourself into failing with negative thoughts?

# Multitracking: Using All the Pathways

Learning is more effective and interesting if it involves as many learning modes as possible. An old proverb about learning goes: *Tell me and I will soon forget, show me and I may remember, let me try, and I will understand.* The truth is listening, seeing, *and* trying is usually better than any one method alone.

Instead of depending on one learning mode, try *multitracking*. Multitracking means to use all the learning modes whenever possible. The brain remembers by being physically stimulated through the senses. The ears, eyes, and movement of the body all stimulate the brain in different ways. By combining these different types of stimulation, we leave a more permanent impression on the brain.

Many people confuse merely being *exposed* to material with being actively involved in the learning. Simply being in the same room and passively listening to a speaker does not guarantee that you have learned anything. You must push yourself to become as actively involved with the new material as possible.

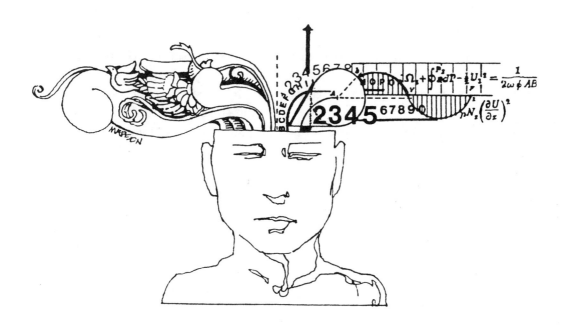

# *To involve all the learning modes:*

**1** **When listening to lectures, examine any and all visual aids.**

Take notes and draw diagrams of what you hear. Ask questions and join in discussions. Volunteer to participate in demonstrations or activities. Work the problems *along with* the math instructor. Use color in your notes to emphasize important points. Recite key points from the class to yourself on the way home. Try anything that will turn a passive "sit and listen" situation into a multitrack learning experience.

**2** **When reading textbooks or manuals, highlight important information.**

Make notes in the margin. Read especially difficult material out loud. Draw diagrams of the new information. Get up and move around occasionally, reciting key points from what you've just read. Write out important points in your notebook. If you can try out the information immediately, do so; this is especially effective when reading a manual for a computer or tool—read and do, do and read. Explain what you have read to anyone who will listen. If possible, teach someone else what you have learned.

**3** **When learning a new job or task, watch a demonstration carefully.**

Ask questions. Ask to try the task yourself. Picture yourself performing the new task perfectly. Ask an expert to observe and critique you. Dig in and try; mistakes are part of learning. If mistakes would be too costly, imitate the process in some less risky way. (Mistakes with a sky diving computer simulator are OK, mistakes while sky diving are not.) Practice. Then practice some more.

## *About Your Thinking Style*

In addition to having a learning style (V, A, or K), people vary in their *thinking* style. We all know people who approach situations and differently than we do. They seem to view the world differently, and even if they reach the same conclusions as we do, they arrive there a very different way.

In the '70s and '80s brain dominance theory became popular and there was a lot of interest in right brain and left brain thinking. While identifying exactly where in the brain a kind of thought process takes place has proven to be much more complex, the fact that people have definite styles of thinking is hard to argue with. In general, the graphic below illustrates the differences in the way the two hemispheres of the brain process information.

*Two Modes of Knowing:*

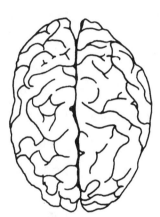

| **Left Hemisphere** | **Right Hemisphere** |
|---|---|
| Logic | Intuition |
| Sequential | Relationships |
| Verbal | Visual |
| Linear | Spacial |
| Analytical | Creative |

Many people overuse one thinking style and under use the other. Some situations call for a very logical, sequential thinking style; others call for a more creative, open style. It is a great advantage to lifelong learners if they can identify when a particular style is appropriate and use tools and techniques that fit the situation. The activity on the next page will help you learn more about your thinking style.

# EXERCISE: THINKING STYLE INVENTORY

For each of the items below, put a check mark (✓) next to the choice that is *most* like you. Check only one choice per item.

1. **When I listen to a song, I pay most attention to the** ❑ words ❑ music

2. **I act on hunches** ❑ seldom ❑ often

3. **I am best at** ❑ word games ❑ physical games

4. **After a movie, I'm most likely to remember the** ❑ actors' lines ❑ visual setting

5. **I like to have my job** ❑ carefully planned ❑ flexible

6. **My closets and shelves are** ❑ well organized ❑ cluttered

7. **I would rather get directions** ❑ out loud ❑ from a map

8. **When putting together something new, I** ❑ read directions first ❑ figure it out myself

9. **I enjoy activities most that are** ❑ mental ❑ physical

10. **I dream** ❑ seldom ❑ often

11. **I like to work on projects** ❑ one by one ❑ several at a time

12. **I am better at** ❑ spelling ❑ art

13. **I daydream** ❑ seldom ❑ often

14. **I try new things** ❑ seldom ❑ often

15. **I prefer to learn by** ❑ listening ❑ doing

16. **I would rather** ❑ explain directions ❑ draw a map

17. **Math is something I** ❑ enjoy ❑ dislike

18. **I pay most attention to** ❑ what people say ❑ how they say it

19. **My sense of direction is** ❑ poor ❑ good

20. **I lose track of time** ❑ seldom ❑ often

**TOTAL** _____ _____

# SCORING THE THINKING STYLE INVENTORY

To score your Thinking Style Inventory, count the number of check marks in each column. The answers in the left column indicate a more sequential, linear thinking style sometimes referred to as "left brained" (logical, straight-line, linguistic). The answers in the right column indicate a more creative, open-ended thinking style sometimes referred to as "right brained" (visual, spatial, less structured, artistic).

When scoring the Thinking Style Inventory, the higher the number in a column, the stronger your preference for that thinking style (left column, left brain; right column, right brain). This is a very short inventory and the results may not be conclusive. However, if there is a difference of more than five between your column totals, you may depend heavily on one style of thinking over the other. The following are suggestions for modifying your style according to the situation.

# Techniques for Modifying Your Thinking Style

## If you need to be more logical and sequential, try:

➤ **Outlining**. It may seem old-fashioned, but it is a great way to organize information.

➤ **Prioritizing**. Decide what is most important, which things should be done first, and what is the most logical sequence to follow.

➤ **Using a schedule book or calendar to keep track of time**. If you see yourself as a free spirit, others may see you as unreliable. Organize your time.

➤ **Making lists**. Lists of things to do can capture your good ideas and make sure they turn into reality.

➤ **Starting projects early and finishing well before the deadline**. Some people consistently underestimate how much time it will take to finish a paper or project and always end up rushing to beat the clock. This decreases the likelihood that they will do their best work and increases the chance of making mistakes.

➤ **Organizing your workspace**. It is very difficult to study or work if you can't find the things you need to do the job. *

➤ **Setting goals with specific deadlines and establishing checkpoints**. This ensures you are progressing at the right pace.

*(For more information on this topic, see Organizing Your Work Space by Odette Pollar, Crisp Publications, 1999.)

## If you need to be more creative and open, try:

➤ **Brainstorming.** By yourself or with a group, come up with as many ideas as possible to solve a problem or approach a task. Don't judge any of the ideas at first, just write them all down. You can sort them out later.

➤ **Drawing a mind map.** A mind map is a free-form outline that shows the connections between ideas and creates a visual image of a body of information. (See page 40.)

➤ **Doing something new and different.** Take an art class or learn a musical instrument. Purposely pick up a magazine you wouldn't normally read and skim a few articles that are outside your normal areas of interest.

➤ **Breaking your routines.** Study in new places, talk to new people. Play a different kind of music in the background when you are trying to be creative.

➤ **Playing the five-sense game.** Try to think in terms of how you can use all your senses to make a project, subject, or idea more interesting. If you are studying history, try to imagine how the Battle of Gettysburg would have smelled. What kind of food did the soldiers eat? What sounds did they hear as they fell asleep? What did the uniforms feel like?

➤ **Reading books or taking courses in creative thinking.** Take a look at *Creativity in Business* (Carol Kinsey Goman, Crisp Publications, 2000).

➤ **Storyboarding your ideas.** Storyboarding is a process that Disney studios originated for laying out animated movies. It also works for writing papers, reports, books, and presentations. First, formulate four or five basic questions that you are trying to answer and write them on 4" x 6" index cards. Then, using 3" x 5" index cards, write only one idea, quote, statistic, fact, or definition per card that addresses the questions you have posed.

# HOW TO STORYBOARD

Stack the idea cards with the relevant question cards. Do not worry about the order of the idea cards right now, just write them down and place in the appropriate stack. If you find information that is interesting or relevant but does not answer one of your basic questions, copy it down on a separate card and start a "miscellaneous" stack. When you have collected more than enough information, spread out your cards so you can look at the big picture.

Now arrange the question cards in the most logical order by deciding in what sequence the questions you have posed should be answered. Line them up at the top of your workspace. Now, arrange each idea cards under the appropriate question card. Move the cards until you are satisfied with the order. Eliminate cards that no longer seem important and add cards from the miscellaneous stack, if appropriate. When you have finished, all you will need to do is write the narrative that will hold your ideas and quotations together.

# DANA: A CASE STUDY

Dana has always been a very energetic, athletic person. She loves to work with her hands and her hobbies are artistic and athletic. In high school, she had little interest in college prep classes but excelled in shop, physical education, and art. She took a job at age 18 as an assembler, putting together specialized electronic components. She quickly mastered more complicated tasks and built a reputation as one of the fastest and most dependable assemblers in the plant. She also has a natural aptitude for fixing technical equipment; when something breaks down, it is often Dana who can get it running again.

At age 28, Dana still likes the company but wants to move into a better-paying supervisory position. She realizes that this will require more education and has started taking an evening class at the community college. Unfortunately, she finds the lecture format and reading assignments involved in her first class boring and time-consuming. She constantly finds excuses to work around the house or yard in order to avoid settling down to study. Dana also finds that she lacks some of the basic writing and study skills that she missed by avoiding college prep classes in high school.

# YOUR ADVICE TO DANA

Pretend you are a close friend or relative of Dana and then answer the questions below.

1.  **What kind of learner do you think Dana is?**
    ❑ **Visual**     ❑ **Auditory**     ❑ **Kinesthetic**

2.  **What advice would you give her about her career?** _____

    _____

    _____

    _____

3.  **How could Dana make learning tasks more compatible with her**

    **learning style?** _____

    _____

    _____

    _____

4.  **Do you have anything in common with Dana? If so, what?** _____

    _____

    _____

    _____

# THE AUTHOR'S ADVICE TO DANA

Dana is a kinesthetic learner: a natural doer, not well designed for the sitting and listening required in formal educational situations. If she decides that supervision is the route that she wants to take, she must face the fact that colleges are designed primarily for auditory and visual learners and that she will have to upgrade her writing and study habits. The sooner she builds those skills, the less likely deficits in these areas will get in her way.

Dana should accept her kinesthetic nature and try to build it into her approach to education. She should do her best to picture herself applying the content of lectures and readings. Creating a vivid image of an activity or situation as she learns about it will make coursework feel more real and appeal to her need for active learning.

Dana should also build activity into her learning routine. She should use her artistic and mechanical ability to turn words into diagrams and pictures in her notetaking. When break time rolls around, she should get up and take a quick walk while mentally reviewing the high points of the previous hour. At home, she should study in short bursts punctuated by even shorter bursts of physical activity. While she will need to sit or stand still to read, she can move around while mentally reviewing material. A child's chalkboard or dry-erase board could be a useful tool for standup review, diagramming, and practice. For kinesthetic learners like Dana, writing, drawing, speaking, and moving should be regular parts of the study routine.

Further, she should explore career alternatives. She may be making the mistake many employees do: "I need to earn more money, so I have to get a degree and go into management." She needs to think about her motives for going to school and for seeking a promotion. If the only reason that she wants to move into management is to earn more money, she may be better off exploring other options. For example, Dana may want to pursue advanced training in specialty soldering or welding, or she may want to apply to an apprenticeship program in a skilled trade. Her aptitude for fixing equipment could be extremely valuable; as the workplace becomes more dependent on gadgets, the people that can keep them running are in great demand. Along with demand comes a higher wage. While supervision may be the way for Dana to go, she needs to think about whether she will be happier "doing things" or managing other people who are "doing things."

# Be Adaptable to the Learning Situation

Besides always being on the lookout for new learning opportunities, to be a successful lifelong learner you must be ready to adapt to different situations. These four common learning situations each require different behaviors and thinking styles from the learner.

## 1 The Traditional Classroom

The instructor talks, gives assignments and tests. The learner needs to be on time, read assignments, take notes, and ask good questions. The traditional classroom frequently puts the learner in what looks like a passive role. But it is not enough merely to attend class. To get the most out of the situation, the learner must be involved and well prepared.

## 2 The Laboratory

The laboratory can be any situation where the learner gets the chance to practice with new information and skills. On-the-job learning is frequently done in a laboratory-type environment where success is a result of curiosity, sharp observation skills, and the willingness to make (and learn from) mistakes. Experience is an excellent teacher, even if some of the experiences are failures.

## 3 The High-Tech Tutors

Computers, VCRs, the Internet, CD ROMs, and audio books provide new ways to sharpen skills and expand knowledge especially when it comes to independent learning. Each technology has its own advantages and challenges. The lifelong learner needs to overcome any reluctance or fear of technology to benefit from available options.

## 4 Experiential Learning

The key requirements for successful self-directed learning are a keen desire to continue growing and improving, the ability to set and reach goals without outside encouragement, understanding how to find necessary information, asking good questions, finding people who can act as mentors, and constantly looking for new learning opportunities.

# *Self-Perception*

There is another important factor that will affect what and how much you learn: your self-perception. By the time you are an adult, you have formed some strong opinions about yourself. Some of these opinions put you in a positive light: "I'm a good parent," or "I can be trusted." Other opinions can limit you, such as: "I'm terrible at math," "I'm just not creative," or "I'm too uncoordinated for that."

While defining and accepting both your strengths and weaknesses can be an asset, beware of negative self-fulfilling prophecies. Many students in math class who have thought "I'm terrible at math" proved themselves right by shutting down at the first challenge presented to them. Frequently, if they do fail, the real reason is not aptitude, but rather that they were not prepared for that particular level of math. Many times adults are not patient enough to start at the level they are ready for and build up to where they want to be. Instead, they expect to compete immediately against golfers who have been playing for years, rebuild a motorcycle engine on the first try or be able to make music on a guitar after a lesson or two.

It is true that most people do have talents in one area and deficits in others. It may take you longer to learn a particular skill than it does someone else, and there may even be some things that you will never master, but the real difference between success and failure at learning is usually time and effort, not inborn ability. Don't write yourself off until you've given it your best.

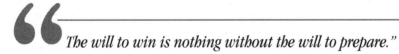

*The will to win is nothing without the will to prepare."*

**–Recent advertisement for an athletic shoe**

# EXERCISE: YOU, LEARNER MIND MAP

This chapter was designed to help you understand yourself better as a learner. Mind mapping is a creative way to organize information. Mind maps are used for planning, organizing, studying, and notetaking. They also work well as memory-assisting devices. They work for most people because they simulate the way the brain is organized. Connections are created between bits of information and organized around a central theme. Each connection can lead the learner back to the central theme or on to another connection. This is how a simple mind map summarizing this chapter might look:

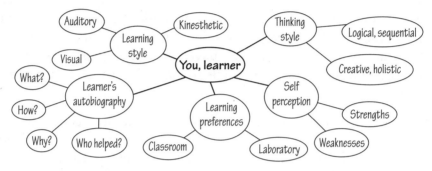

## Now, you try it:

In the space provided, draw your own mind map of what you found out about yourself as a learner. Start with your name in a circle at the center and use the branches to describe you, the learner.

# Improving Listening, Memory, and Reading Skills

# Tactic 4: Using "Brain Friendly" Learning Techniques

Understanding a little about how your brain learns can make learning easier and more enjoyable. It isn't necessary to understand the physiology of the brain to improve how you learn, but it is important to understand how what you do externally translates into learning internally.

## *There are three general principles that nearly all learning appears to be based on:*

**1** **The importance of concentration and attention in absorbing new information**

**2** **The role of association and patterns in the storage and recall of information**

**3** **The value of repetition and practice to mastering new knowledge and skills**

Most experts now agree that thought, memory, and even emotion are the result of a combination of electrical and chemical activity in the brain and the rest of the nervous system. Each neuron (brain cell) communicates with other neurons by way of signals that cross tiny gaps between nerve cells called synapses.

When you think, remember, or even experience an emotion, a complex process of signals travels between the neurons in your brain. These signals physically change your brain, making connections between different brain cells. In a very real sense, the better "connected" your brain is, the smarter you are. You can continue to make new connections throughout your life; therefore, barring disease, you can continue to get smarter throughout your life.

This chapter will show you practical ways to form more and better connections when you listen, read, or try to memorize information. These fairly simple strategies can have a profound impact on the inner workings of your brain.

## *Concentration/Attention*

Every year dozens of articles are printed on the topics of listening, reading, and studying that give very good advice that is nearly impossible to follow. The advice tells you to *make* yourself pay attention—concentrate, avoid being distracted, and focus on main ideas.

This type of advice is given to students and business people all the time. What these people are really being asked to do is to "pay attention to their attention," a skill that very few people have completely mastered. Meditation is about paying attention to your attention, and anybody that has tried to meditate can tell you how truly difficult that can be. Being aware of whether or not you are concentrating is even harder.

### If I Could Only Concentrate!

Concentration is at the heart of listening, reading, studying, and learning successfully. When you say that you haven't been listening, you are merely saying that you haven't been concentrating on what was said. When you say you didn't comprehend what you just read, you are often admitting that you just didn't concentrate.

Concentration is hard to master because it usually comes as a by-product of doing something interesting. If you are doing something that truly engages you, you have no trouble concentrating. However, it is often hard to begin concentrating on a topic if it doesn't immediately grab your interest. Any new input (a book, a lecture, someone's name) must compete for your attention.

To see just how hard it is to control your own mind, try this little experiment:

Close your eyes and *try not to think of anything* for just one minute.

Tough, isn't it? Your brain seeks stimulation, and, if nothing is happening externally to stimulate it, it will find something internally to think about. Random thoughts, memories, and wishes race through your brain for no apparent reason, interfering with your ability to listen, read, and commit information to memory.

What we need is a different approach to thinking about concentration; an approach based on a quote from philosopher and educator William James:

"We are more likely to act ourselves into feeling, than we are to feel our way into acting."

Here's an idea: perhaps our internal state (inattention, depression, happiness, concentration) is the result of external behaviors, not the other way around. Instead of, "I was doodling in class because I was bored," maybe "I was bored because I was doodling!" Instead of, "I take lousy notes because I hate history," maybe "I hate history because I take lousy notes!" Instead of, "I didn't finish the report because I'm depressed," maybe "I am depressed because I didn't finish the report!"

This may not sound like a radical idea at first, but it does give you a fresh way to approach concentration problems. Instead of *thinking* about concentrating harder, you should *behave* in ways that will help you concentrate. By being prepared, acting interested, and getting involved in a class, your ability to concentrate will be greatly improved. Don't wait to be in the mood to concentrate; don't wait for the topic to grab you. Get started and act interested—often your enthusiasm will grow *as a result* of your actions.

Can't get started on a paper? Make yourself write for five minutes, anything that relates to the topic. Not interested in a chapter you need to read? Make yourself skim the chapter, looking intently at all illustrations, dark type, charts, or graphs. Worried about remembering names? Make yourself repeat the names carefully when you first hear them. Act interested, and you will often become interested!

*(For more on this topic, see <u>Concentration: How to Focus for Success</u> by Sam Horn, Crisp Publications, 1991.)*

## Associations and Patterns

There is a myth that your memory has limited capacity and will some day simply "fill up." But memory is not like a box or drawer; in fact, the more the brain is used, the more you learn, the more connections you make in the brain. Therefore, the more connections you make, the more connections you are able to make, and the easier it is to find and use information. Our brain is more like a scaffold, or a Tinker Toy structure than a box; you can add to this memory network throughout your entire life, each new item you add connecting to existing ones.

Making associations and connections is a critical part of learning. Connecting new information to something that you already know is an essential part of successful learning. That's one reason that it is easier to learn more about something you already have some knowledge of than it is to start on a completely different field. As you listen, read, or try to memorize material, and the more you consciously try to connect information to what you already know, the easier it is to store and retrieve when you need it.

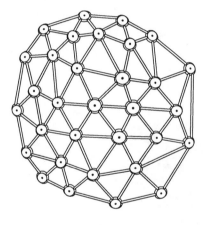

## Repetition and Practice

Practice may not always make perfect, but it will almost always make better. Your brain must decide what to remember and what to forget. There are just too many stimuli in an average day to remember everything. One factor that influences what you remember is how many times and for how long you pay attention to something.

A joke that you hear only once and don't think about again is quickly forgotten; a joke that you repeat in your mind and then tell several times is remembered. A name that you hear once or twice is often forgotten; a name that you use several times in conversation and write down is remembered. A word that you look up today, you may have to look up again a month from now, but a word that you look up and then use is quickly committed to memory. There is no substitute for practice.

# Tactic 5: Learning to Listen, Listening to Learn

## *Productive Listening*

Your daily life is filled with what could be passive listening experiences. Students attend lectures; employees attend meetings. You spend countless hours in situations where one or two people do the talking and the rest are supposed to soak it up. This idea contradicts the way people learn: people learn by being active users of new information, not passive hearers.

Productive listening starts by understanding ourselves and the listening process. Communication is a complex act of moving information from one human brain to another by converting ideas into words in the speaker's mind and converting those words back into ideas in the listener's mind. Since words have multiple meanings and can be strung together in less-than-perfect sentences, the opportunities for misunderstanding are great.

Before you can understand another person's words, those words must pass through many "communication filters" or distractions. These distractions can alter or sometimes even block the original meaning of the message. Some distractions you are very aware of, like the noise in the room next door or the voice of the impolite whisperer two seats over. You may not, however, be aware of others. The listening distraction inventory that follows is designed to help you become aware of those things that tend to distract you the most.

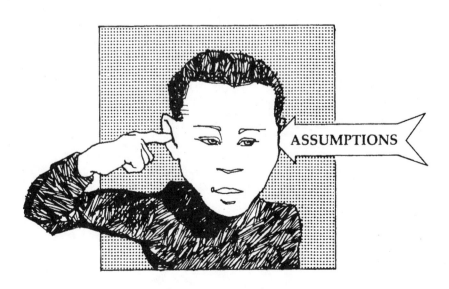

ASSUMPTIONS

48

# EXERCISE: LISTENING DISTRACTION INVENTORY

Read through the entire list below and then rank in order the following factors according to how much they distract you when you are trying to listen. Use the number 1 to indicate the factor that distracts you the most, 5 to indicate the factor that distracts you the least. Rank only your top five.

A. _____ Noise and activity in the immediate area

B. _____ A speaker with an unpleasant voice

C. _____ Profanity

D. _____ Ideas that are different from your own

E. _____ Dress style or hair style that is very different from your own

F. _____ Your own internal thoughts and concerns

G. _____ A large age difference between you and the speaker

H. _____ An accent that is different from your own

I. _____ A speaker who "talks down to you"

J. _____ A disorganized speaker

K. _____ Prior negative experience with the speaker

# *Battling Your Personal Distractions*

By becoming aware of those things that distract you the most, you can better prepare to address your own biases and weak spots. Below are tips for each of the distractions on the survey. Focus on your top five personal distractions.

## TIP 1: Noise and activity in the immediate area

Do what you can to control distractions by taking a quiet seat and limiting your view of people and activity. If you cannot control the distraction, acknowledge that it exists and then focus on your listening, not the distraction. If you have trouble seeing or hearing what is going on in a class, get there early enough next time to pick a prime seat.

## TIP 2: A speaker with an unpleasant voice

Listen for content, not style. Many very informative people have a strange voice or poor public speaking skills. The more you think about how much the professor sounds like a cartoon character, the less you will hear or retain content.

## TIP 3: Profanity

Some people think that the use of profanity makes their message more powerful. However, research has shown that some people so dislike swearing that they don't hear any of the message. If you are listening to someone who has a habit of using off-color language, try to focus on content, not word choice; if you are truly offended, you may need to raise your concerns with the speaker.

## TIP 4: Ideas that are different from your own

Learning is about exposing yourself to new ideas. You do not have to change your mind in order to listen to and understand another point of view. Try comparing and contrasting your own ideas with the speaker's instead of resisting the new information. You will be better equipped to defend your position if you understand the other side.

## TIP 5: Dress style or hair style very different from your own

Although society has become much more open about style, most of us still have our own expectations surrounding appearance. Be open. Many brilliant teachers have worn funny-looking clothes or styled their hair in an unconventional way.

### TIP 6: Your own internal thoughts and concerns

Do everything you can to become actively involved in listening. If you still find your mind is wandering, pull yourself back to the lecture by writing down the last thing that you remember hearing. It may help to jot down unrelated concerns so that you can free your mind up to focus on the task at hand. Avoid getting frustrated with your wandering mind; instead, *gently* refocus.

### TIP 7: An age difference between you and the speaker

"That young pup" or "that old fogy" are both examples of age prejudice. People often place too much importance on age and not enough on knowledge. Knowledge and wisdom can come from a person of any age.

### TIP 8: An accent that is different from your own

Many scholars from other countries teach in the United States. If you have trouble with a person's accent, try to relax. Accents can be more difficult to understand if you try too hard. Don't be afraid to ask when you do not understand something; most instructors want to make themselves understood and will be glad to help you. If you continue to have trouble, form notetaking teams with other students and compare notes after class.

### TIP 9: A speaker who "talks down to you" or "above your head"

Most of the time, the slight is unintentional. Many people are truly unaware of how they sound. People who have studied a topic for many years use language that they think is basic when, in fact, beginning students may not understand it; or they assume you won't understand and insult you with simplistic explanations. The best tactic is to be prepared. Read assignments and memorize new vocabulary for the subject before class, ask questions when you don't understand, and form a notetaking team for your class.

### TIP 10: A disorganized speaker

Again, the best advice is to be prepared: read assignments and memorize new terms beforehand. Ask when you don't understand something, and form a notetaking team for your class. Your questions can sometimes help the speaker stay "on topic." Leave plenty of extra blank space in your notes for filling in ideas in case the instructor skips around.

## TIP 11: Prior negative experience with the speaker

It is possible for learners to have an unresolved conflict with an instructor, but unless you can choose another instructor, remember to focus on your reason for being in the class, not on who the instructor is. If you fail to learn, you are the one who loses.

## BILL: A CASE STUDY

Bill has been working on a college degree at night for two years. When he gets to class at 7 P.M. he is already tired from a day's work. Bill's job as a manager is one that he has trouble leaving behind. Today, his boss told him he has to cut another 5% from his already tight operating budget.

On the nights that he takes statistics he barely has enough time to stop home and grab something to eat. Tonight, as he rushed out of the house, his wife told him that his son's teacher had sent a note home about a failing grade. Bill promised to deal with it later.

After spending 10 minutes looking for a place to park, Bill rushed in late and got the last seat, by the door near the noisy hallway. He hadn't looked at his statistics homework since last week's class and had a sinking feeling when the graduate student began explaining new material. He strained to understand the instructor's accent and wondered whether a teacher that young could really know what she was talking about. As the problem was written on the board he thought, "I hate math. I never was any good at this stuff."

The student in front of him reminded him of an employee that he had to lay off and he thought of the budget. A voice in the hallway sounded like his son and he thought of the failing grade.

What advice would you give Bill?

# YOUR ADVICE TO BILL

Pretend you are a close friend or relative of Bill and then answer the questions below.

**How can Bill improve his ability to listen in class?** _____

_____

_____


**Is Bill's schedule realistic? What could he do to make it more manageable?**

_____

_____


**Do you have anything in common with Bill? If so, what?** _____

_____

_____

# THE AUTHOR'S ADVICE TO BILL

If Bill has made a good choice in pursuing his degree at this stage of his life, then he must accept the realities of his world and the challenge of this statistics class. If this is a required course, then Bill has a very clear goal: pass the class and leave with as much useful knowledge as possible. He certainly won't want to drop the class (a waste of time) or fail (a waste of time, money and ego). Bill needs to accept the class and recognize how it fits into his goals.

Bill should not rush home for dinner on class nights. Instead he should pack a meal and eat somewhere on campus. He should leave work at quitting time and head straight for campus. Parking on campus is usually much easier between 4 P.M. and 6 P.M. after the day-student rush and before the evening-student rush. He should find a spot to eat and study that is quiet enough to review his notes and look over this week's material.

Bill should get to class early and take the best seat in the house, about three rows back and in the center of the room. This will put him directly in the instructor's line of sight and close enough to understand what is said. It will also get him away from that noisy hallway. The other students who sit in the front will tend to be the ones most interested in the course. They will be good to get to know to review notes with or to form study groups.

Bill should write out any questions he has about the homework. Almost all math instructors start class by asking, "Were there any questions about the homework?" Bill should have also checked the syllabus (course outline) to see what will be covered during that class.

He should try hard mentally to become a student and put work and home on the back burner. If thoughts about work or home persist, he should write them down to address after class. Writing problems down will help put them out of his mind for now by assuring him that the issues won't be forgotten.

It is important for Bill to relax and focus on the material, not the age, gender, or accent of the instructor. If he relaxes and tries, he will get better at understanding accented speech. If Bill still can't understand, he must ask. If he doesn't want to interrupt, he can mark the spot in his notes with a question mark and later ask the instructor or a fellow student for help.

Immediate review is the best kind of review. After class, Bill should take at least 10 minutes to correct and complete his notes and begin one problem from the homework. This 10 minutes could save hours trying to remember how to do the problem. It will also help to imprint the new material on his memory.

# Listening as a Three-Stage Process

Aggressive listening can be very demanding. If you are listening in an important situation at work, in a class, or at home, you should look at listening as a three-stage process:

**Stage 1: Making the mental transition to listening**

**Stage 2: Making the physical transition to listening**

**Stage 3: Engagement with the speaker**

Each of these stages involves a series of simple steps, a kind of "listening checklist." There is no way to devise an exact formula for every listening situation. Just remember, when you are listening to produce results of some kind (to make a sale, to pass a test, to complete a project), you should run through the listening checklist. With effort and practice this new approach to productive listening will become automatic.

## *Stage 1: Making the Mental Transition (R.E.A.D.Y.)*

The first stage of effective listening should happen before the conversation or class even starts. This stage prepares you mentally for what you will hear. By shifting your attention before the communication begins, you will be better prepared to understand the message. Just remember the acronym R.E.A.D.Y. (An acronym is a memory device that uses the first letter of several words to form a clue word.)

**R**eview

**E**liminate

**A**nticipate

**D**etermine

**Y**ank

# Review your last contact with the speaker

When possible, prepare for your role as listener by reviewing the last time you listened to that same person. One of the best ways to get the most out of a class is to review the lecture notes from the last class. This will focus your mind and prepare you to follow the flow of today's lecture.

# Eliminate controllable distractions

Select a seat away from noisy hallways and impolite people. Set yourself up to focus on the information at hand. Put away any papers or books that may compete for your attention. Sit where it is easy to see the instructor and hard to see anything that may distract you.

# Anticipate, but don't prejudge

Try to think ahead of the speaker, but don't be surprised if the lecture goes in a different direction than you expected. Thinking ahead makes you an active participant in the lecture. Reading assignments carefully before a lecture also gives you a head start.

# Determine your listening objectives

Know why you are listening. Go into the class, seminar or meeting with questions in mind that you hope will be answered. Keep in mind why you decided to attend. Even if this is a required class that holds little interest for you now, remember how it will help you reach a long-term goal.

# Yank yourself into the present

All too often, learners bring their bodies to a seminar, meeting or class, but their minds are elsewhere. Don't fool yourself. In order to learn, you must focus on the moment that you are in. Adult learners have busy lives and a lot on their minds, but it's a waste of time to worry about yesterday or tomorrow and miss what's going on now. Be here, now.

## *Stage 2: Making the Physical Transition (S.W.A.T.)*

The second stage shows you how to assume the correct listening posture for a lecture or meeting. This is the simplest and perhaps single most powerful part of the three-stage process.

The nonverbal messages that you send by physically preparing to listen almost always improve communication by showing the speaker that you are really interested. In addition, this posture sends the message to your own brain that you are there to listen and learn.

### Sit up and lean slightly forward

This is an alert posture that helps inspire an alert mind. Leaning back or slouching invites sleepiness and makes notetaking more difficult.

### Watch as well as listen

By keeping an eye on the instructor, you will pick up additional information through visual aids, body language, gestures, and facial expressions.

### Acknowledge what you hear

Use nods, facial expressions, and questions.

Communication is a continuous loop; how you listen affects how someone speaks. The positive feedback of an attentive audience improves the quality of a lecture. More importantly, these outward expressions of interest help convince your own mind to concentrate.

### Take notes

Although sometimes it feels like notetaking is distracting, a written record of a seminar or lecture will last much longer than your memory will. Especially if you are going to be tested, well-organized notes are essential. *

---

*Lengefeld, Uelaine. *Study Skills Strategies*. Crisp Publications, 1994

# Stage 3: Engagement with the Speaker (F.A.R.)

Now you are mentally and physically ready. In the third stage you will learn how to keep listening actively. To listen actively, you must take measures to ensure that you continue to follow the speaker's train of thought.

## Focus

Concentrate on the content of the lecture, not the instructor's appearance, accent, tone of voice, or personality. Many instructors or bosses are not skilled public speakers. Remember why you are in the class or meeting: to gain and refine your skills and knowledge. Increase your involvement by nodding when you understand, involving yourself in discussions, and picturing yourself applying the content of the lecture. Imagine yourself in a one-to-one conversation with the instructor and use the same kind of focused attention you would when listening to your best friend.

## Abbreviate

Take notes and don't worry about spelling, correct grammar or neatness. As long as you can read and understand your notes at a later time, they will serve their purpose. Leave plenty of white space between topics and at the end of lines. This blank space will come in handy later when you fill in details and complete your thoughts. Leave a blank column on the left side of the page for markers, symbols, and important terms.

## Revise

Whenever possible, revise and refine your notes within 20 minutes after class. Make this a routine that you strictly follow. This revision session helps to capture new information before you forget it.

# Tactic 6: Making the Most of Memory

## *Mnemonics: Association and Visualization*

In the last section on listening, you were introduced to three acronyms to help you remember the three stages of the listening process. Do you remember what they were?

In the spaces below, write the three acronyms and as much as you can remember about what they stand for.

**Making the Mental Transition**

**Making the Physical Transition**

**Engagement with the Speaker**

The acronyms that you just reviewed are a type of mnemonic. Mnemonics are techniques for improving memory, formed with visual images, rhythm, rhyme, association, or connections to previously learned material.

## Some examples of mnemonic devices:

**i before e except after c**
> using rhythm and rhyme to remember a spelling rule

**Every good boy does fine**
> connecting first letters of words in a phrase with lines on a musical score

**H. O. M. E. S.**
> for remembering the Great Lakes—Huron, Ontario, Michigan, Erie, Superior—acronym and association

**Many Very Early Maps Just Show Us Nine Planets**
> to remember planets in order from the sun—Mercury, Venus, Earth, Mars, Jupiter, Saturn, Uranus, Neptune, Pluto—using a sentence to remember the sequence of items in a list

**SPA. Socrates, Plato, Aristotle**
> to help remember the names of three Greek philosophers that had teacher-pupil relationships and who taught whom

If you had trouble remembering the mnemonics for the listening process, go back and study them for just a few minutes. You'll be surprised at how much you remember with just a little concentrated effort. You can also create mnemonics yourself.

# *The Name Game*

One very common and frustrating learning task is recalling new names. "I'm terrible at remembering names," people say, "but I never forget a face."

## Remembering names can be challenging because...

➤ You are often distracted by external noise and activity while you are being introduced to someone new.

➤ You are often distracted by *internal* noise; you're so busy thinking about what you will say next that you don't pay attention to the person's name.

➤ Your memory may be overloaded by having too many new names to remember at once.

➤ Names often sound meaningless—at first glance, names like Bob, Sue, and Frank have little meaning. If you think about those names, however, each word has a meaning in a different context.

➤ You often live *down* to your own self-fulfilling prophecy of being terrible at remembering names.

When you meet someone new, try playing the name game by creating a meaning for the new name. Here's how it works:

1. Listen carefully to the name to find a meaning. For example, "Bob" means to bounce up and down, "Sue" is something that happens in a courtroom, and "Frank" means to be direct and honest. With a name like Alice, which does not have an obvious meaning, play "sounds like," (e.g., Alice sounds like A-List).

2. Create an image of an object or action that the name sounds like, involving the person you have just met. (Picture Bob bouncing up and down on a trampoline.)

3. Repeat the name as soon as possible and then again at the end of the conversation.

4. Concentrate on the details of the person's face while mentally reviewing the name.

# EXERCISE: THE NAME GAME

Try playing the name game right now with the names of people you already know. You might even try it with your own name, just for fun. List three names below and search them for meaning. If they have no obvious meaning, play "sounds like" with the name. Finally, picture the person's face in great detail. Do they wear glasses? What color is their hair? Their eyes? What is their most distinguishing feature? If you go through this process with people that you have just met, you will find that your capacity for remembering names and faces increases greatly. Try creating an image to go with the first and last name.

**Name** _____

**Sounds like** _____

**Description** _____

_____


**Name** _____

**Sounds like** _____

**Description** _____

_____


**Name** _____

**Sounds like** _____

**Description** _____

_____

## *Beat the Forgetting Curve*

Even when you want to remember new information, you will often forget. That is because forgetting is a natural, predictable process, which begins as soon as learning takes place. New information is lost rapidly, especially in the first 20 minutes. If not reviewed, between 70% and 90% of new information can be lost within 24 hours. Psychologists call this pattern of rapid information loss the "forgetting curve."

### Follow these tips to interrupt the natural forgetting process:

- ❏ **If you want to remember something, review it immediately, and then again within 20 minutes.**

- ❏ **Break long study sessions into 20-minute blocks followed by five-minute review sessions.**

- ❏ **Use a spaced-practice schedule. 20 minutes a day for five days is much better than two hours at one sitting.**

- ❏ **Make the information meaningful. Don't try to memorize information that you don't understand.**

- ❏ **Organize information into chunks of seven items or less. Studies have shown that seven is the maximum number of items that the average person can hold in short-term memory. If you must memorize a long list of 25 items, divide it into four smaller lists grouped in some logical fashion.**

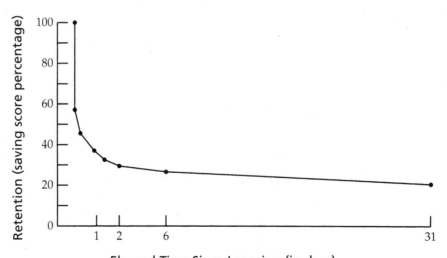

## *Your Powerful Visual Memory*

Visual memory is usually more powerful than your memory for words, numbers, or sounds. Unfortunately, much of what you are expected to memorize isn't visual. Facts, numbers, and names do not provide easy-to-remember images like faces, scenery, and pictures. When it is not possible to turn the information into real pictures, creating mental images can do the same thing. Practice making "funny mental pictures" to help you remember new information. The more outlandish the image you create, the easier it will be to remember.

# Processing New Information

Studying should be more than just reading, and learning should be more interesting than repetition of information. When studying, switch modes of thinking and interacting with the new material. Don't just read it—say it, listen to it, write it, and make mental images for it. The more ways you can process it, the better.

## Modes you can use to "process" new information are:

- ❑ Visualize it—see it in full color, see it working.
- ❑ Say it into a tape recorder and play it back as you commute.
- ❑ Draw a diagram of it.
- ❑ Sing it.
- ❑ Debate it or explain it to a friend.
- ❑ Make up an acronym or a mnemonic.
- ❑ Rhyme it.
- ❑ Relate it to a past experience.
- ❑ Imagine how you might use it in the future.
- ❑ Make flash cards.
- ❑ Organize it in several different ways.
- ❑ Make up a story using key elements of the information.
- ❑ Outline it.
- ❑ Write in the book.
- ❑ Use a highlighter.
- ❑ Make a mind map connecting related ideas.

# *Memory and Aging*

Many changes come with aging. The good news for lifelong learners is that loss of memory is not necessarily one of them. Some health conditions impact memory, but for the most part, people continue to learn and remember new information throughout their lives. There are changes that aging brings which may affect your ability to learn, but by being aware of these changes, it is possible to compensate for them.

## Weakening of Sight, Hearing, and the Other Senses

The eyesight and hearing usually decline with age. If new information does not make a clear impression on the senses, it is not the fault of memory when the information can't be recalled. Regular vision and hearing tests will keep these changes from sneaking up on you. Hearing and vision can often be corrected or adapted for by carefully choosing where you sit in a room or asking people to speak louder if you cannot hear.

## General Health

The condition of the mind is directly related to the condition of the body. Exercise, rest and good nutrition are important for high-functioning memory and thinking skills. One of the best ways to stay sharp mentally is to stay sharp physically. The brain depends on oxygen, which is delivered through the blood stream. Both aerobic exercise and a low fat diet will help keep the blood vessels to the brain unobstructed.

## Speed of Recall

Reaction time slows with aging, including the time it takes to recall information— but the decline is a gradual one. After 50, it may take a little longer to respond to questions. But whatever adults lose in speed is generally made up for in knowledge. The anxiety of not remembering a name or a date immediately often makes the problem worse. Relax, and it will usually come back to you.

## Retention

If what they learn is meaningful and interesting, older people retain information just as well as younger people. The real issue behind retention of new information is whether you pay attention in the same way you did when you were younger. Snowfall might not have the magic it did when you were eight; your fiftieth trip to the lake isn't as exciting as your first. You don't pay as much attention, because the experience is not as fresh. The more routine your day is, the harder it is to remember the details of that day. To keep learning, try to surround yourself with new and interesting activities and people. Search for personal meaning and opportunities for application in the new information and experiences that you encounter.

When caring for an older family member or friend, don't assume diminished mental capabilities or be afraid to suggest breaking their routine. Artists, authors, political leaders, and business people often stay active and highly involved into their 70's, 80's and beyond. These people have stayed engaged with the world around them instead of allowing their worlds to shrink.

## Distraction

Background noise and nearby conversations tend to become more distracting as you age. This change begins as early as 30 and becomes more evident as you get older. Teenagers are famous for thriving in a multisensory environment, often reading, listening to the radio, and talking on the phone at the same time. While this may be somewhat distracting at 16, it is absolutely chaotic at 60. A clean, quiet, organized workplace is an asset to any age, but may become a necessity as you get older. If you find you have trouble focusing on a conversation in a busy environment, try moving it to a quieter space.

# External Memory Aids

Memory techniques are not meant to replace the use of external memory aids, tools that people have created to help you remember. Calendars, files, lists, and electronic reminders can remove much of the burden from your memory and the chance from your daily life.

## Calendars

A calendar should both tell you about today and warn you about upcoming events for which you need to prepare. A reminder on April 15 that taxes are due may be too little too late. To be effective, the tax reminder should appear earlier, perhaps on March 15 with the note: taxes due one month, get to work.

## Lists

Creating lists and following through on them is one of the most efficient aids to memory and time management. Set aside time to create a daily list and then refer to it several times throughout the day to stay on track and to add new items. The feeling of accomplishment that comes from checking off completed tasks can act as a built-in reward system for getting things done.

## Pick-Up Points

It is very frustrating to get to work and realize that the report you were supposed to submit is at home on the kitchen table. Get in the habit of creating a consistent pick-up point at home and at work. Put what you need at the pick-up point as soon as you think of it. The thought may not come again. Possible pick-up points: on the table by the door, on a mantle, or on top of a file cabinet. Make it a habit to always check your pick-up point before leaving.

## Do Something Different (Ticklers)

When it occurs to you that you need to stop on the way home and buy a birthday card, do something "different" right when the thought occurs. Put your ring on the other hand, put your watch on upside down, put a paper clip on your key ring. Every time you notice that something is different, it will tickle your memory and should remind you of what you need to do. This is the old string-on-the-finger trick.

### Time Savers

Consistent habits save time. You will never spend time looking for your keys if you always put them in the same place. You won't hunt for phone messages if you have one notebook where you write down all your messages. If a file folder is re-filed correctly after each use, it will be there when you need it. Habits are hard to change, but it is worth the effort to become a better-organized person.

### Electronic Helpers

A wide variety of handheld computerized tools are available to help you keep track of names, phone numbers, appointments, special dates, etc. Even watches can be set to remind you when it's time to go.

### Take Notes

When in doubt, write it down. Then you can give your full attention to what is at hand. The weakest ink is better than the strongest memory.

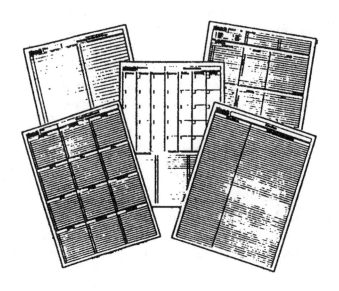

# Time Management and Memory

Don't blame your memory for problems that are really caused by your own poor time management. Hurrying causes you to forget things you would ordinarily remember.

## Here are some tips to manage your time:

➤ **Build both a planning time and a wrap-up time into your daily schedule.** A few quiet moments to think ahead in the morning and a few moments at the end of the day before leaving work will do wonders to ensure that important details are not forgotten.

➤ **Live in the present.** Planning for the future is important, but being preoccupied with either the past or the future will lead to missing out on what is going on now.

➤ **Allow transition time between activities.** Put things where they belong, write a date on your calendar, and think over new information. Rushing from task to task can cause errors.

➤ **Arrive ahead of time for appointments and meetings.** The stress of being late can interfere with your ability to remember. Spend the extra time preparing for the meeting. Avoid over-committing, which makes it impossible to be on time.

➤ **Build time into your life for physical activity and fun.**

## *Additional Strategies*

If you need help, here are some additional memory improvement strategies:

➤ **Make sure you hear or see the new information correctly.** If it doesn't register with your senses or you get it wrong to start with, you cannot possibly retrieve or apply it correctly.

➤ **Pay attention.** You remember what you focus on. Much of what happens around you is lost simply because you did not pay attention. This is the number one reason that people forget names.

➤ **Review.** Think about, picture, repeat, write, or say new information within 15 seconds, if possible. Review again within 20 minutes. Mentally repeating what you want to remember signals the brain that this information is valuable. The more ways you review new information, the more likely you are to remember. This is especially true when trying to remember names.

➤ **Organize information.** The better information is organized when you try to study, the easier it will be to remember. You can use a traditional outline to organize, or a mind map to show all the connections between bits of information.

➤ **Use your imagination and have fun.** The mind remembers creative, interesting, ridiculous, colorful images best. If you can make vivid associations with boring information, that image will become your retrieval device.

➤ **Relax.** It is harder to learn when you are stressed.

# Tactic 7: Learning from Printed Materials—Reading

It's not high-tech, it's not fancy, but reading is still the most portable, versatile, and flexible way to gather new information. While there are thousands of instructional videos and computer programs on the market, there are millions of books, magazines, and manuals. Whatever the topic, something has been printed about it. Being an effective reader is still one of the most powerful and inexpensive ways to be a lifelong learner.

Even though reading is universally taught in our society, it is not universally mastered. Even proficient readers sometimes find themselves in the frustrating position of needing to re-read material. Reading can become so automatic that even though you hear the individual words in your head, the meaning of what you read may escape you; and the *meaning* is what is important.

The key to reading comprehension is to become mentally involved with the print so that you are always thinking about what you are reading. *Reading is thought, guided by print.* Usually when readers face a comprehension problem, they blame the book. They say it's too boring, too hard, or poorly written. However, nothing can be done about the book if it is one you must read. Reading is the learner's job and a skilled reader can often make up for a boring author.

The two main causes for poor reading comprehension are a passive reading style and poor concentration. To learn from printed material, your mind must be focused and your reading style must be aggressive. How well you remember what you read depends on the intensity of the work you do on the information.

To read aggressively, you need a system. Try the following four-step approach, Learner Centered Reading, to increase your comprehension.

> " *Reading is a dynamic act, the creative coming together of minds."*
>
> **—Waldo Frank**

# Learner Centered Reading: a Four-Step Process

## STEP 1: Consider What You Know

To focus your concentration at the beginning of a reading session, you must first link what you already know with what you are about to read. Look over the title of the chapter and read the first paragraph of a new reading assignment. Think about previous material that led up to this section. Write down a few things that you already know about the topic.

## STEP 2: Predict What You'll Learn

Anticipating or predicting what comes next will prepare your mind to receive new information. Pose a series of questions to yourself that you believe should be answered by the text, then consider reading as the act of looking for the answers.

Begin each session by previewing a section that you can read in the space of about 20 minutes. Look over all bold-faced type, charts, graphs, or illustrations, then pick a few sentences at random and read them. At the end of your preview, stop and write down a few predictions about what you are about to read. What questions should you be able to answer by the end of this section?

## STEP 3: Read Aggressively

Always read with a pen in your hand. Underline, make notes, write in the margins. If you cannot write in the book, make notes of important pages in your notebook. Use symbols and diagrams to emphasize information that you need to remember. If preparing for a test, mark the passages that look like logical choices for test questions.

## STEP 4: Review and Summarize

At the end of each 20-minute reading block, review what you have read. Test yourself to see what you have retained. Without looking at the book, summarize the material. Start the summary with the words, "I learned. . ." For example, "I learned that the start-up sequence for operating the Supercomplex Robotic Widget Maker is…" Stopping to summarize helps both comprehension and memory.

# EXERCISE: LEARNER CENTERED READING

Use this page to practice learner centered reading. Pick out a selection of material that you can read in about 20 minutes and follow the steps below.

1. **Look at the title and first paragraph then write a summary of what you already know about this topic. Tie the information to any previous readings or classes.**

   *I know* _____

   _____

   _____

2. **Look over all bold type, diagrams or illustrations and then predict what you are about to learn. Generate at least four questions that you should be able to answer after reading.**

   *I predict* _____

   _____

   _____

3. **Read and make sure your thoughts are guided by what you read. Underline, make notes, and use symbols as you read. If you cannot mark in the book, make a simple outline of the content.**

4. **When you have finished reading, write down what you have learned without looking back at the selection.**

   *I learned* _____

   _____

   _____

   _____

# *Improving Your Concentration When Reading*

Reading, like most tasks, requires concentration. To improve your ability to concentrate when reading, follow these tips.

## TIP 1: Set the Scene

Eliminate as many distractions as possible. Make sure you are getting adequate rest, a good diet, and enough exercise. Finally, try to concentrate in short bursts of 15–20 minutes at a time. These short bursts of study are much more effective than four-hour cram sessions.

## TIP 2: Use a Timer

You may want to buy a timer to prevent clock watching and help you create an achievable goal. To begin, set the timer for five or ten minutes. Make yourself focus on reading until the buzzer goes off. At the end of the time, take a short break—about one minute of break for every five minutes of concentration.

## TIP 3: Take a Break

Build up until you can concentrate for 20–25 minutes and earn a five-minute break. At the end of the break, begin the process again. At the end of third 20-minute session, you may want to reward yourself with a longer break or a treat of some kind.

## TIP 4: Review and Summarize

Finish each session by reviewing what you have learned. Write a short summary and review important details, including charts, headings, and your own notes and markings.

## TIP 5: Act the Part

Sometimes you may not want to read even though you need to. If that's the case, force yourself to *pretend* to concentrate. Move to your study area, preview the material, set your timer, and *act* like you are concentrating. Often all you need is the willpower to start. Once the brain is engaged, real concentration will take over. If you wait until you are in the mood, you may never start.

# Making Technology, Habits, and Experience Work for You

# Tactic 8: New Learning Technology

Today's world is filled with tools to help enrich and expand when, where, and how you learn. No longer is the learner limited to the printed page or the lecture hall. No longer is the library a place that specializes only in books. Audiotapes, videotapes, CD ROMs, the Internet, and computer programs all bring the power of technology to the act of learning.

Many schools, colleges, and companies are investing heavily in high-tech learning equipment. Home computers, the Internet, VCRs, and audiotape recorders also make it possible to take advantage of these advances at home, while you travel, and even in your car. By becoming familiar and comfortable with these learning tools, you can expand your learning options, increase the time you devote to self-improvement, and add valuable technology-related skills to your list of abilities.

This section includes an overview of a variety of high-tech learning tools and provides advice for getting the most out of each type of technology.

## *Audiotape*

Bookstores and libraries now have entire sections devoted to books on tape (audiotaped versions of printed materials either in full-length or condensed forms). Originally, taped books were created for people with visual impairments or reading difficulties. Gradually, a market developed for busy people who want to "read" as they commute, paint the bedroom, exercise, or mow the grass. Audiotape has become a real alternative to print for many people.

### Advantages of Audiotape

- ✓ **Great for auditory learners**

- ✓ **Helps fill commute time**

- ✓ **You can listen to a "book" and still be mobile**

- ✓ **Provides an alternative to reading for those who don't like to read or have trouble reading**

- ✓ **With the instructor's permission, you can use a tape recorder to capture entire lectures to review as you commute or work around the house. (This is a very time-consuming way to review and should be used only when lectures are too difficult to summarize in the form of good comprehensive notes.)**

## Limitations of Audiotape

Taped books are clumsy. It is impossible to skim with audiotape, and to repeat a section you must rewind, find the spot you want, then replay the tape. You also can't underline or highlight a cassette and there are no graphs, pictures, or maps to fall back on for clarification. In addition, the spoken reading voice is much slower than most people can read.

## GETTING THE MOST FROM AUDIOTAPE

To help overcome the natural limitations of listening to taped books, try the following:

❑ Stop the tape and repeat aloud important ideas and facts that you would like to remember.

❑ Make notes during or soon after your listening session.

❑ Listen to important or difficult-to-understand tapes more than once.

❑ If the tape comes with a printed workbook or study guide, use it! Preview the print before listening and stop the tape when you need to look at a chart or answer questions.

❑ Make sure that your recorder has a counter so you can mark where important information will be found.

❑ Consider buying a variable speed tape player that allows you to speed up tapes to a more challenging pace. Special machines are available that can speed up the tape without making it sound funny.

# *Video and Videotape*

Videotape has become part of everyday life. Many families now own a VCR and many have their own video cameras. Video has largely replaced film in the classroom because it is easy to use and handle. Like movies, videos make it possible to see other places and other times. They also make it possible to watch experts or actors demonstrate things such as how to put on a roof, solve a conflict, sell a car, or repair a piece of equipment.

Libraries lend both entertainment and educational videos, or you can buy tapes to have on hand to use whenever you like. In the workplace, companies are beginning to use video-based training because of the flexibility and relative cost-effectiveness of having experts on tape. Because it is feasible to have one student in the room at a time, video makes it possible to train only the people who need it, when they need it.

## Advantages of Videotape

✓ **Great for visual learners**

✓ **A picture is worth a thousand words**

✓ **Great for demonstrating physical skills**

✓ **Easy to use at home**

✓ **Can be slowed down, replayed, and reviewed**

✓ **Can help pace instruction to an individual's speed**

✓ **The TV generation is comfortable with video**

✓ **Available day or night for classes of one to 1,000**

✓ **Video can be used as a feedback tool (e.g., reviewing a tape of yourself performing a skill, or seeing and hearing yourself give a speech). This works even better if you review the tape with an expert coach**

## Limitations of Videotape

The biggest problem with video is that it looks and sounds too much like entertainment TV. Learners frequently settle into a classic TV-viewing mode, which can be pretty passive. Using video also means that you need two pieces of equipment, the VCR and the monitor (TV). Furthermore, since video is expensive to produce, production companies must make their product general enough to appeal to the widest possible market. While the content of a video may remain sound, many videos quickly become dated by the dress or hair styles of the cast. Lastly, like audiotape, it is difficult to skim or review video; much time can be wasted rewinding and searching if a very comprehensive guide is not provided.

# GETTING THE MOST
# FROM VIDEOTAPE

- ❑ Be selective. Many companies make preview sample tapes available at no cost or commitment. The quality of educational video varies drastically. Don't waste time on a video that doesn't truly serve your purpose.

- ❑ Treat video like a class. Take notes, answer questions that are asked, and become actively involved.

- ❑ Look for videos with extensive print support in the form of workbooks, quizzes, and study guides.

- ❑ Preview all printed material.

- ❑ Remember, educational video only looks like commercial TV. Don't be fooled into a passive approach.

- ❑ Take frequent breaks if you are losing your concentration.

- ❑ If the video is part of a class, don't hesitate to ask the instructor for clarification. If you don't want to interrupt, write your questions down to ask at the end.

- ❑ Use the counter to note where important information is located on the tape.

# *Computer Based Training (CBT)*

CD ROMs and DVDs work very much like a musical compact disc (CD). A beam of light (laser) reads the information on the disc and produces pictures and sounds on a video monitor. The monitor is usually connected to a computer keyboard or has a touch screen. Disc technology is better than tape because a disc need not run straight from beginning to end. The machine can find any information on the disc quickly, either at the direction of the user or as a response to an answer. This ability is what makes the learning truly interactive.

Well-programmed discs can steer learners according to their interests and abilities. A math lesson will analyze the learner's mistakes and try to identify a common weakness such as inability to multiply fractions. The disc will then suggest (and sometimes insist) that a review of the skill should be completed before going further.

Another example of this flexibility: a lesson may use a "branching technique." This presents a situation and asks the learner to choose from a preset list of possible actions. By choosing an option, the student is guided through one of several possible scenarios. By tracking the learner's responses, the program can present material in a personalized order and at the appropriate speed, becoming a highly flexible and personalized tutor.

## Advantages of Computer Based Training (CBT)

Interactive software shares all the advantages of traditional videotape, plus:

- ✓ CD ROMs and DVDs combine the power of video and the speed of computers

- ✓ It is possible to integrate multiple forms of media like text, audio, video, and animation. This provides variety and gives learners a way to use the visual, auditory, and kinesthetic pathways to the brain

- ✓ It is possible to access information almost instantly from any place on the disc

- ✓ Pictures are usually sharper using disc technology

- ✓ Better CBT systems and programs allow the learner to access the content in any order instead of following one set, linear path like audio and videotape

- ✓ Provides access to huge pools of information

- ✓ Can be paced to the learner's speed and ability

- ✓ Is an endlessly patient teacher

- ✓ No need to be embarrassed by what you don't know

- ✓ Learner can start class anytime of the day or night

- ✓ Good programs will not review what you already know or start over your head

- ✓ With the right equipment, you can learn whenever and wherever you want

## Limitations of Computer Based Training

A disadvantage for some students is the absence of human interaction. While it is possible to design a total learning experience that considers the need for human interaction, CD ROM and DVD are usually used by individuals in isolation. Further, as with all instruction that is costly to program and produce, CD ROMs and DVDs frequently become outdated long before they can be replaced. As old-fashioned as a professor's lecture notes may seem, it is still much easier to update a lecture than most of these high-tech tools. This is a critical consideration when selecting training materials in rapidly changing fields.

## GETTING THE MOST FROM COMPUTER BASED TRAINING

❏ Becoming comfortable with the equipment is the number one requirement for getting the most out of this technology.

❏ Interactive disc technology is still a less common tool than audio and videotape. Look for the opportunity to work with this type of teaching aid, and, when you find it, become oriented to its mechanics. Most of the better programs will guide you through the process.

# Web Based Training

Web Based Training (WBT) is similar to Computer Based Training (CBT) except that it delivers the content over the Internet or an organization's intranet via a computer with access to the Web. Usually, learners will need to be signed up for the training to receive a password and gain access to the website.

Like Computer Based Training, WBT can use a wide variety of media, including print, sound, video, and animation. If you have the right equipment and access to the training, you can use it at any time, in any place in the world. Companies with employees in different locations can save on travel costs by offering training over the Web. Learners have the advantage of attending "class" without leaving the cubicle, office, or home. Because Web Based Training is easy to update, the content can be kept more current. Current and future improvements to computer technology will allow Web Based Training to get even better, faster, and more interactive with improved graphics and sound.

## Advantages of Web Based Training

In addition to all the advantages of CBT,

- ✓ **WBT combines the power of video, the speed of computers, and the access of the Internet**

- ✓ **The multitracking nature of WBT makes it a good fit for all learning styles**

- ✓ **Encourages active participation in the training**

- ✓ **Provides access to material for large numbers of learners in many different places**

- ✓ **Learners can interact with instructors and each other, regardless of location**

## Limitations of Web Based Training

WBT shares some of the limitations as Computer Based Training, especially the lack of face-to-face interaction with instructors and other learners. The initial cost of equipment and the restricted access of much WBT can also be prohibitive.

## GETTING THE MOST
## FROM WEB BASED TRAINING

❑   Just like other forms of learning that involve computers, you must get comfortable with the technology involved.

❑   WBT is best when combined with other forms of learning including print, video, and classroom interaction.

## *The Internet*

Of all the new media, the Internet is causing the most change in the way people learn, interact, research, and communicate. This change has been so rapid that the first edition of this book did not even mention the Net. One hot new trend is the "live Internet classroom" where students and teachers in different locations interact in real time, just like in a traditional classroom setting.

There are books that focus exclusively on navigating the Internet, but if you are interested in reading up before you get started, buy one with a very recent copyright date.

Perhaps the best way to learn the Net is to go exploring. Most colleges and universities now have a presence on the World Wide Web where you can access information about courses and majors, apply, register, and even take classes online. Further, many communities also have web pages that keep residents informed about all types of events, including free seminars and classes. If you would like a specific destination to get started, try the Crisp Publications website at *www.crisplearning.com*, where you'll find information on hundreds of self-study materials that can support your lifelong learning goals.

### Advantages of the Internet

✓ **Provides access to huge pools of information**

✓ **Almost every topic can be found on the Net**

✓ **No need to be embarrassed about what you don't know**

✓ **Access the whole world from your home, school, or office**

✓ **Provides a chance to interact with other people interested in the same topics no matter where in the world they live**

✓ **This is truly a two-way medium, post your questions, join a chat group, build a web page, send instant messages across the globe**

## Limitations of the Internet

You'll need a computer, a modem, an Internet Service Provider (ISP) and a phone line (a dedicated one is best). Or, you can just go down to the public library and use its system. Once you are online, finding what you need can be tricky because you may have to sort through some pretty worthless stuff. It is easy to get overloaded with information, but it is just a matter of practice to learn how to do a decent search. Remember the focus of what you were looking for and be careful not to get "hooked."

The best use of the Internet may be as a research tool, but because anybody can post anything on the Internet, always verify information before believing it; hoaxes, scams, and outright lies are daily pitfalls of the medium. Depending on the speed of your modem and the size of the pipe (phone or cable line) that you have, downloading information can be as slow as mud.

## GETTING THE MOST FROM THE INTERNET

- ❑ **Unless you have plenty of time, it is best to know specifically what you are looking for before signing on**

- ❑ **Do a few just-for-fun searches on a hobby or interest to get the feel for how things work**

- ❑ **When possible, ask the experts (usually 14- to 20-year-olds) for advice about how to use the medium**

- ❑ **If you want more detailed instruction, buy a book specifically about getting around on the Internet.**

# Tactic 9: Make the Power of Habit Work for You

**Habit Definition:** _____

*an acquired pattern of behavior that has become almost involuntary as a result of frequent repetition.*

Habits are often seen as things that you need to "break." The truth is, the right kinds of habits can have a powerful positive effect on your life. You've heard that exercise and good nutrition will improve your health, appearance, and energy level. Most people have tried to exercise more and eat better at some time in their lives, but many have found that changing behavior for a day or two, or even a week or two, doesn't make much difference.

However, small changes, that become habits, can have a tremendous impact. When you repeat an activity on a daily basis so that it becomes almost automatic, you are guaranteed to see the effects. The couch potato who starts taking a brisk 20-minute walk every day will see a real change in a couple of months. The person who invests $20 a week every week will be impressed by how much they save in a couple of years.

The same is true of the person who makes the A.S.K. attitude a habit. There may not be a lot of difference in you at the end of the first day, or even the first week. But a month from now, a year from now, five years from now, there will be a significant increase in what you know and what you are able to do. And along with that difference may come a new job, new interests, a promotion, or just an increased sense of confidence and self-worth. But first, you have to form the habit of being an assertive, mindful, lifelong learner.

## How You Can Form a New Habit

Start by remembering the "Rule of 3's":

❑ **after 3 days of consistent practice, a new behavior will start to become a routine**

❑ **after 3 weeks of following a routine, you will have started to form a new habit**

❑ **after 3 months, the new habit will become part of "who you are"**

During the first 2 phases of habit development, a break in your new routine of more than a few days can send you right back to square one. Once you get to the "3 month" phase, the habit will have a life of its own. The Rule of 3's works in forming habits of all kinds, good and bad, habits that relate to health, wealth, friendship, and knowledge. It is the cumulative affect of actions, repeated on a consistent basis, which will determine your future. If people are really creatures of habit, they better make sure they are good habits.

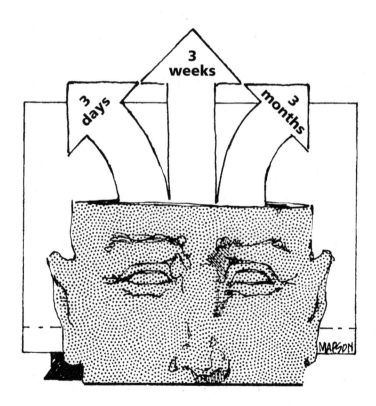

# EXERCISE: HABIT INVENTORY

Think a minute about your habits, especially the ones that have an impact on your learning (what you read, how you spend your leisure time, how you act toward new challenges on the job or at home), then answer the questions below.

**List three current habits that you believe support your efforts at being a lifelong learner.**

_____

_____

_____

**List three current habits that may interfere with the goal of being a lifelong learner.**

_____

_____

_____

**List three habits that you would like to develop that would support the future that you want.**

_____

_____

_____

## *Pay Attention to What You Pay Attention to*

Hundreds of television channels, shelves full of magazines, daily newspapers, thousands of web sites, stores full of videos, radio talk shows, music programs, and news broadcasts. Classes offered at work, in hotel meeting rooms, at local schools, the Y, and even at bookstores. New technology being introduced every day, updated versions of software replacing earlier versions that you haven't mastered yet. It gets down to this: you have only so much time and so much attention to spend in a day, a week, a life. In a very real way, what you pay attention to is what you learn, and, to a certain extent, what you become.

Time and attention are the two most limited resources of modern life, and life-long learners must use them wisely. If you make bad decisions about how to spend your time and attention, there's no way to replace them. There is nothing wrong with watching a TV show just to be entertained, reading a novel just for fun or staying up all night "surfing" the Net with no real plan. Every once in a while, significant learning can even happen that way. Real entertainment or recreation can have a significant learning value of its own; truly enjoying something can be as important to a balanced life as learning something new. But watching a rerun you've seen twice before? Reading a dozen books in which nothing changes but the names? Browsing the Web and looking at unimportant sites like "Dave's Home Page" featuring his personal collection of beer cans?

## Vary Your "Information Diet"

What you listen to, watch, and read can become habitual. Even if you are fairly selective and watch "good" TV, read the editorial page of the newspaper, and subscribe to magazines in your field of interest, you can still become intellectually malnourished if your information diet isn't varied and well balanced.

Try to vary your sources of information. Whatever your political interests, listen to commentators from the other side every so often. When you travel, try picking up a local paper instead of that national one. If you usually listen to the classic rock station on the way home from work, try the local alternative station, or better yet, quality news and information programs that can be excellent sources of information on a wide range of topics.

Do you have a set of encyclopedias or an encyclopedia program for your computer? Flip (or click) through it randomly, stopping now and then to read whatever catches your attention. Talk to different people at work or school, watch someone else do their job for a while, and ask them a few questions. Even in the doctor's office or on an airplane, pick up a magazine you usually would not read to pass the time. You might discover a new interest.

Each of these activities will open up new avenues of learning that you can choose to explore. You'll be surprised at what interests you if given the chance. You'll also begin to see patterns and connections that you never new existed. Becoming well-rounded will help you to put your learning goals into a broader context, and will also enable you to carry on conversations on a greater number of topics, ask better questions, and think about things more clearly.

You'll also notice your vocabulary grow, and, since words are the building blocks of thought, you'll find you can think more clearly as you learn how to use more words correctly. Keep a good dictionary on hand to look up words you don't know or are unsure of. Even one word a day will make a difference. If you focus your vocabulary building on a particular field, you'll see the benefits even faster.

## Cut Down on Empty "Intellectual Calories"

Are you wondering when you'll find the time to spend on lifelong learning? Good question. Just like it is hard to eat right if you first fill up with junk food, it is hard to find time to learn if your free time is taken up with empty intellectual calories. Look for times in your regular schedule when you are doing little besides killing time. Most people won't admit that there is such time in their regular day, but you might be surprised. Completing the learning activities that follow will give you a better sense of where your time goes.

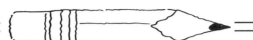

# EXERCISE: BIOLOGICAL CLOCK

## Identify Your Prime Time

Everyone has a biological rhythm to the day; times when you feel more energetic and other times you have trouble staying awake. If you can identify your "prime time" and make it a habit to schedule learning tasks for those times, you will be working with your body instead of against it. Answer the questions below to help identify your own prime time.

Do you consider yourself a ❑ morning person or ❑ night owl?

What time of day is your energy level the highest? _____

What time of day is your energy level the lowest? _____

When do you concentrate best? _____

Do you feel like you need a nap at a particular time of day? If so, when?

_____

Left completely to your natural schedule, what time would you go to bed at night? _____

Left completely to your natural schedule, what time would you get up in the morning? _____

Based on your answers, place a check mark (✓) by your prime times, that is, when you feel the most alert. Then, indicate your "slack time," that is, when you feel the least alert, with an X. You may select more than one time period for each.

❑ Early morning (5 to 8 AM)            ❑ Early evening (6 to 8 PM)

❑ Mid morning  (8 to 10 AM)           ❑ Mid evening (8 to 10 PM)

❑ Late morning (10 AM to Noon)        ❑ Late evening (10 PM to midnight)

❑ Early afternoon (Noon to 2 PM)      ❑ Early overnight (midnight to 2 AM)

❑ Mid afternoon (2 to 4 PM)           ❑ Middle of the night (2 AM to 5 AM)

❑ Late afternoon (4 to 6 PM)

# A Time to Learn

Applying the information about your biological clock is simple. Learning requires you to be mentally alert; the more demanding the learning, the more alert you need to be. Whenever possible, schedule learning tasks during your prime time and avoid them during your slack time. This is especially true when setting aside time to read. Reading is a fairly passive activity and makes many people sleepy if they try to do it when their energy level is low. Also, avoid scheduling lecture classes during low energy times of day.

## What if Your Prime Time is Outside Your Normal Schedule?

You may find that your prime learning time is outside your normal schedule. Many people who live and work in a busy environment find that very early in the morning before the rest of the house is awake or late at night after others have gone to bed offer the most distraction-free times. Just don't make the mistake of thinking you can get by with less rest than you need—a tired brain loses much of its sharpness. Some adults try to postpone learning until everything else is done; the problem is, everything else is *never* done. Learning time must be a priority.

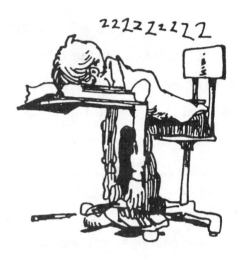

# A Place to Learn

You have rooms for eating, rooms for sleeping, family rooms, some people even have a TV room. But do you have a place to learn? Having a place that is conducive to learning can be the difference between concentrating and daydreaming, between getting down to work or wasting time. While learning can and will occur anywhere, having a special space where your primary role is "learner" can be a great asset.

First, if at all possible, your learning place should be used solely for that purpose. Set up a spare bedroom, a corner of the basement, or any other area that can be used exclusively as your study area. If this is not possible, at least move out of the normal traffic pattern in your home or go to a library.

## Ask yourself these questions about your learning space:

1. **Is the level of sound comfortable to you?** ❏ Yes ❏ No
   Silence is golden for some people, others need a little background noise. If you can't find a completely quiet place, consider using soft instrumental music such as classical or light jazz to mask the noise in the environment. Studies have shown that Baroque classical appears to be the best, but any music without lyrics that helps you concentrate will do.

2. **Do you have all the supplies that you will need?** ❏ Yes ❏ No
   A well-stocked study area should have pens, paper, tape, rulers, stapler, typing or computer supplies, and basic reference books such as a good dictionary and thesaurus. As you focus your interests, you may want to start your own private library of related reference materials.

3. **Is it reasonably (but not too) comfortable?** ❏ Yes ❏ No
   You should be comfortable, but alert. Being comfortable is good, but trying to read while lying down is just asking for a nap. If sleepiness is a frequent problem for you, try studying standing up. Thomas Jefferson and Ernest Hemingway both read and wrote that way.

4. **Is it fairly uncluttered?** ❏ Yes ❏ No
   A learning place should have some sense of order to it. Try to limit the material on your workspace to what you are using and develop a filing system for materials that you want to keep.

5. **Is the light good enough?** ❏ Yes ❏ No
   Experiment with several lamps and bulb strengths to get the right amount of light. Over-the-shoulder light is best for reading.

6. **Does it encourage you to work?** ❏ Yes ❏ No
   The atmosphere should be appealing and stimulating. There should be a sense that "this is a place I can focus."

If you answered "no" to any of the above questions, what can you do about it? Is your area fixable, or do you have to find a new place of study? If no place in your home is adequate, consider carrying a special "learning briefcase" that includes all your supplies. You may find that your best study area is a library, an empty classroom on a campus, or even an office after work hours.

# Habits that Promote Lifelong Learning

Below are a few habits that support the goal of being a lifelong learner. Try to build as many of these habits into your life as possible.

- ❑ Looking for and taking on new challenges
- ❑ Reading, and reading some more
- ❑ Listening to news and informational radio
- ❑ Listening to instructional cassettes
- ❑ Exploring new technologies, especially learning about the Internet
- ❑ Talking to different people, especially people you don't always agree with
- ❑ Varying your routine
- ❑ Visiting libraries and museums
- ❑ Saying yes (within reason) when you're asked "Would you like to try...?"
- ❑ Saying no to reruns
- ❑ Learning new words
- ❑ Taking classes and/or attending training
- ❑ Trying new hobbies
- ❑ Asking "Can I try that?"
- ❑ Traveling to new and interesting places
- ❑ Getting familiar with the public and educational channels on the TV
- ❑ Using the off button on the TV remote
- ❑ Volunteering
- ❑ Getting in "over your head"
- ❑ Looking up words you aren't sure of
- ❑ Flipping through the dictionary or encyclopedia and randomly reading the entries

# Tactic 10: Experiential Learning

## *Experience: The Best Teacher?*

You've heard the expression, "You learn from experience." That saying is partly true. Every day life presents opportunities to learn from experiences, whether you take advantage of those opportunities is a different story. Have you ever made the same "dumb mistake" more than once? Ever done the same painful thing more than once? It may be because you *didn't* learn from your earlier experience.

You learn from experience when you think critically about those experiences. Even mistakes (maybe especially mistakes) can provide valuable learning insights if you employ a simple concept called the *Experiential Learning Cycle*. The Experiential Learning Cycle consists of asking and answering three questions as they relate to a particular event or experience.

➤ **"What happened?"**

➤ **"So what does that mean?"**

➤ **"Now what will I do in the future based on this experience?"**

Say, for example, you made a bad decision buying a used car and ended up paying too much for a car with serious mechanical problems. How could you turn that negative experience into a positive learning opportunity? Let's take those questions one at a time to see how the process works.

### "What happened?"

This is both a factual and analytical question that makes you think about all the factors involved in the event. Did you wait until the old car quit running before starting to look for a new one? Did you take a stranger's word for something that you should have had checked out by a mechanic you trusted? Did you do adequate research on the blue book value and the model's strengths and weaknesses?

### "So what does that mean?"

When you look at the facts of the situation, what conclusions can you draw? Did you pay too much for the car? If so, about how much? Should you have bought a different car? What would have been better? Is there anything you can do to correct your mistake this time?

### "Now what will I do in the future based on this experience?"

This is the pay-off question. How will you apply what you learned to future situations? What will you do differently as a result of thinking critically about this experience? What will you do the same? There are probably lessons that apply to more situations than buying a car. How can you link what you learned to other areas of your life?

You can use the Experiential Learning Cycle to analyze any experience, positive or negative, trivial or significant. Making a mistake buying a used car once, is simply that—a mistake. Making the same kind of mistake again may show a pattern of faulty thinking that needs to be addressed. Learning from your every-day experience can be an extremely valuable tool in lifelong learning.

## *Using the Experiential Learning Cycle to Improve Relationships*

Do you want to improve your relationship with your boss, a co-worker, or even a family member? After each interaction with that person, ask yourself the questions above and see what you discover. You may be surprised at the results.

# Action Learning

One of the best ways to learn is to seek out and take on new challenges and try things that you've never tried before. This is called *action learning*, and, when combined with the Experiential Learning Cycle questions, it is a powerful tool for self-development.

Action learning means to jump into a new challenge and learn by doing. Never done any public speaking? One way to start is to volunteer to talk before a community group or club and deliver a presentation on a subject that interests you. Toastmasters, an international organization dedicated to teaching public speaking, uses the "learn by doing" premise to help thousands of people a year polish their speaking skills.

Don't know much about the Internet? Jump in and research an issue online. You may need a little help to get started, but you'll be surprised how much you learn as you go. If you don't have a computer or access to the Internet from home, go to the public library and get online there. The reference librarians are glad to help.

## Your Present Job as a Great Source of Action Learning

Keep your ears open for challenging projects at work. According to the Center for Creative Leadership, successful managers and executives say that completing challenging assignments accounted for 42% of their learning/development, a much higher percentage than they attribute to classroom instruction (under 15%). You can also support your action learning with a variety of self-study materials including books, tapes, videos, and computer-assisted instruction.

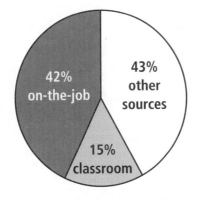

*42% of learning is achieved through on-the-job assignments*

## EXERCISE: EXPERIENTIAL LEARNING CYCLE JOURNAL

Start keeping a journal of what you learn from your daily life. Use the three questions of the Experiential Learning Cycle to guide your writing:

➤ **"What happened?"**

➤ **"So what does that mean?"**

➤ **"Now what will I do in the future based on this experience?"**

Remember that this is a journal, not a diary. Use it only as a record of what you are learning. You may or may not make an entry every day, but the more often you do, the more it will reinforce your efforts to seek out learning opportunities. A simple spiral notebook will do to record your notes, or, if you carry a day planner or calendar, you can use the notes section to do your journaling. You can also use your journal to keep track of your vocabulary development activities.

Remember the Rule of 3's of habit formation. It will take you at least three weeks to get into a real routine with your journal, but it will be worth it.

# *Learning On The Job*

Opportunities to learn at work are growing dramatically. Nearly every organization is encouraging, even demanding, that employees continue to expand their knowledge and skills. Unfortunately, many people see this as a threat.

## As a lifelong learner at work, you should:

❑ **Look at employer sponsored learning opportunities as a win-win situation.** Your employer gets a better-educated, more flexible employee and you gain more marketable skills. Your employer becomes more efficient and, presumably, more stable. You become a more valuable employee with a more stable firm, and also gain the greater personal freedom of increasing your options in the job market.

❑ **Find out about your employer's formal educational programs and take advantage of them.** Your company may cover all or part of the cost of taking classes. Educational benefits are the least-used of all the fringe benefits offered to employees; literally billions of dollars go unspent each year. Enroll in seminars and classes offered through the workplace.

❑ **Let your supervisor know that you are interested in upgrading your skills at work.** Ask to be trained on new equipment or to learn new job functions. If you are interested in greater responsibility, become more flexible by mastering new skills.

❑ **Find a mentor.** Look around for someone who has skills and knowledge that you would like to gain. Tell that person that you are interested in learning what they know. Ask for advice, direction and help.

❑ **Ask questions.** Keeping your weaknesses secret or covering up what you don't know will usually cause you more problems in the long run. If you think there may be negative consequences to telling your supervisor about a skill deficit, seek help at a community college, university, or vocational school.

## JOE: A CASE STUDY

Joe has worked in the same medium-sized manufacturing plant for 21 years. He has been a supervisor for the last 10 years. Until recently, he had complete decision-making power for ordering supplies, scheduling work, and assigning overtime. Recently, the company hired two young computer wizards to select computers and design programs to help make some of those decisions. They frequently use computer jargon in conversation that sounds like a foreign language to Joe.

Joe feels as though he is losing much of his authority and the computers intimidate him. He has never had the opportunity to learn about computer-assisted manufacturing, and is afraid of looking stupid in front of the new employees. He is so uncomfortable with the changes around him that he is considering looking for a new job.

What advice would you give Joe?

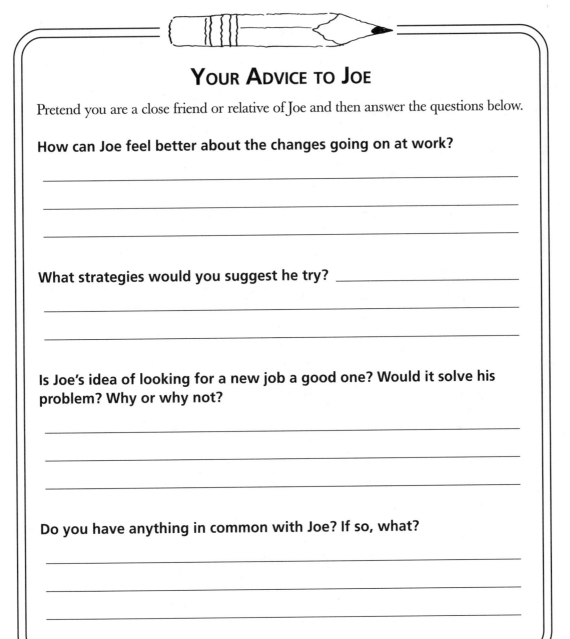

# YOUR ADVICE TO JOE

Pretend you are a close friend or relative of Joe and then answer the questions below.

**How can Joe feel better about the changes going on at work?**

_____

_____

_____

**What strategies would you suggest he try?** _____

_____

_____

**Is Joe's idea of looking for a new job a good one? Would it solve his problem? Why or why not?**

_____

_____

_____

**Do you have anything in common with Joe? If so, what?**

_____

_____

_____

## THE AUTHOR'S ADVICE TO JOE

Whether Joe realizes it or not, the new computer programs could help him and make his job easier. He should ask his supervisors to be included in the planning stages of computerization, because the input should come from people who will use the system. Joe should request that he meet regularly with the programmers so that all relevant information he has gained through experience is included.

At meetings to plan for the computerization, Joe should ask how the employees are to be trained on the equipment, how the equipment works, and what the goals are for its use. Joe is probably not the only person threatened by new technology. He can ask to be trained first and can then help set up training for others under his supervision.

As Joe talks to the programmers, he should ask them for explanations when he doesn't understand their jargon. He probably doesn't need to take an outside class, because the equipment and program at his job will be industry- and job-specific, but developing an interest in how computers work generally will be useful. Finally, if Joe seriously believes he can escape the computer revolution by changing jobs, he is mistaken; it is best if he faces his concerns now, rather than trying to run from them.

# Conclusion: Lifelong Learning Options

Lifelong learning is becoming a big industry; many educational options are available to you as a lifelong learner. Some of the more common types of programs are described here. Be careful when selecting any program or provider of education. Like any field where there is money to be made, the level of quality and integrity varies greatly in the learning industry. Check out several options and make an informed choice. Remember, advisors at both public colleges and for-profit schools are selling their particular product. Before making any commitment, make sure what they are selling is right for you. The following pages list some options for you to explore.

## Adult Basic Education

Programs designed to help adults master basic literacy and mathematics skills. Often offered through the public school system, they may lead to earning a General Equivalency Diploma (GED), the equivalent of a high school diploma earned by passing a series of tests.

## Independent Study

Learning on your own with no formal school, instructor, or program. Can be done through books, tapes, video, hobbies, friends, travel, observation, jobs, the Internet, etc. It is the most flexible, least structured path to lifelong learning, but offers no credentials to verify accomplishments. Many colleges and universities now offer programs that give credit for prior independent learning. Keep records of your independent self-study in the event you ever want the credentials.

## Seminars

Offered through colleges, high schools, community centers, or companies. Many are conducted at work on company time. They range in length from a few hours to several days. Many are offered in public locations like hotels or conference centers. Most offer informal proof of completion such as a certificate, and some are approved for Continuing Education Units (CEUs). Be sure to keep records of your seminar attendance for possible portfolio credit or to be included in your personnel file.

## Correspondence Study

Correspondence study is individual instruction by mail or over the Internet. Students can enroll any time, study at home, and set their own pace. Work is typically guided on one-to-one basis with a faculty expert who designs materials, guides the students, and grades or otherwise responds to student work. Both noncredit and credit programs are offered through correspondence. Credit can be earned at any level from elementary school through graduate programs.

## Adult school

Programs range from diploma completion classes to hobby courses. Some classes are designed to teach job-related skills that will help students find specific types of employment, others are "learning for its own sake" classes.

## Certificate Program

Generally defined as one or more technical courses completed in one to 26 weeks. Normally each program focuses on one particular skill area. Graduates receive a certificate verifying completion.

## Diploma Program

A program offering technical and basic coursework. The program generally requires 600–1,500 hours or 40–90 quarter credit hours. Graduates receive a diploma upon completion.

## Associate Degree

Community and junior colleges offer an Associate Degree or two-year degree, which refers to the length of time most programs would take a student to complete if going to school full time. Programs include technical, basic, and general courses.

## Bachelor Degree

The basic degree offered by four-year colleges and universities. Students declare a major area of study and also complete general education requirements. These days, most students in four-year programs take longer than that to complete their course of study.

## Graduate Programs

Programs begun after completion of a bachelor degree that lead to a Master, Specialist, or Doctorate degree.

# GLORIA: A CASE STUDY

Gloria is a single mother of two children, works full-time at a local hospital as a practical nurse, manages the household, and spends as much time with her children as possible. She also lives in the same city as her aging parents and tries to help them out when they need her. She is living on a very modest income and knows that she and the children will need a larger paycheck as years go by.

Gloria knows that the registered nurses she works with make much better money than she does. She has talked to several of them and found that most of the new nurses have bachelor's degrees. She had a brief conversation with a university advisor and was shocked at how long it would take to finish a degree in nursing. She has also talked to the other nurses about the difficulty of the program, and they advised her that there were many hours of study involved. Since it has been 10 years since she last was in school, she doubts her ability to keep up.

Her goal of earning a better paycheck by becoming a registered nurse seems almost impossible with the demands of family and job. She is very discouraged.

# YOUR ADVICE TO GLORIA

Pretend you are a close friend or relative of Gloria and then answer the questions below.

**How can Gloria sort out her educational options?**

_____

_____

_____

**What are the roadblocks to Gloria pursuing an education? How can she overcome those roadblocks?**

_____

_____

_____

**Is Gloria's schedule realistic? Could she do anything to make it more manageable?**

_____

_____

_____

**Do you have anything in common with Gloria? If so, what?**

_____

_____

_____

# The Author's Advice to Gloria

Gloria's situation is not unique. For many people, lifelong learning is not a luxury, but a matter of economic survival. Gloria needs to think and plan very carefully to ensure that she makes good decisions about her goals.

**To explore her options more carefully, Gloria should:**

➤ talk to her supervisors, the personnel office, and other employees about her avenues for earning more money

➤ contact other employees to understand their needs and find out about opportunities outside the hospital

➤ create as long a list of options as possible including job change, overtime, learning a specialized skill, working premium replacement hours (weekends and evenings when others don't want to work), or going to school to prepare for a job change

➤ consider taking a career exploration course through a local community college or other source

Gloria may find that she can be trained for another skilled position that will help her earn a better paycheck and require less preparation time than becoming an RN. If she does decide that becoming a registered nurse is the best option for her, she should now explore as many different ways of reaching that goal as possible. Is a bachelor's degree really required? Will it bring the highest pay? Do hospitals in the area hire nurses from associate degree programs? From diploma programs? Are there any special programs to help practical nurses become registered nurses more quickly? What school is the most flexible in scheduling classes?

Only after this exploration stage is completed should Gloria commit to a direction to take. If she does go back to school, the planning process is not over. She must consider childcare, when and where she will study, and how she will finance her education. The more planning she does, the less chance she has of frustration, discouragement, and dropping out. Many special programs and services are offered at the local level to help adults in situations like Gloria's and she needs to find out about them. Gloria's road won't be easy, but if she doesn't start on it, she could find herself in the same situation five years from now.

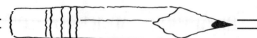

# EXERCISE: YOUR CASE STUDY

### The First Entry in Your Learning Journal

Now it is time for you to start your lifelong learner's journal. You can use a notebook, journal, or personal computer. Keep records of your thoughts, ideas, and accomplishments as a lifelong learner.

At the beginning of your journal, write a short case study like those you have read in this book. Include a description of your situation, goals, skills, attitudes, and possible obstacles that you face. When you have finished, put your case study aside for a week. At the end of a week, read it again and then write out your advice to yourself. Base your advice on the material in this book and your own thinking. This activity will serve both as a review of what you have learned and an opportunity for reflection.

After thinking of your current situation, go back to Your Learning Goals Work Sheet on page 13. Are your goals still valid? If so, what have you done to make them a reality? Based on that goal sheet and the other ideas in this book, begin to build your Lifelong Learning Action Plan.

# EXERCISE: ACTION PLAN

What are the first five steps or tasks you will take on the path of lifelong learning?

When will you begin?

|  | Goal | Tasks | Deadline |
|---|---|---|---|
| 1. | _____ | _____ | _____ |
|  | _____ | _____ | _____ |

|  | Goal | Tasks | Deadline |
|---|---|---|---|
| 2. | _____ | _____ | _____ |
|  | _____ | _____ | _____ |

|  | Goal | Tasks | Deadline |
|---|---|---|---|
| 3. | _____ | _____ | _____ |
|  | _____ | _____ | _____ |

|  | Goal | Tasks | Deadline |
|---|---|---|---|
| 4. | _____ | _____ | _____ |
|  | _____ | _____ | _____ |

|  | Goal | Tasks | Deadline |
|---|---|---|---|
| 5. | _____ | _____ | _____ |
|  | _____ | _____ | _____ |

*Good luck and good learning!*

# Related Readings

Bowles, Richard. *Three Boxes of Life*. Berkeley: Ten Speed Press, 1999.

Burley-Allen, Madelyn. *Memory Skills in Business*. Menlo Park, CA: Crisp Publications, 1988.

Ellis, David. *Becoming a Master Student*. Boston: Houghton Mifflin, 1998.

Edwards, Betty. *Drawing on the Right Side of the Brain*. New York: Jeremy P. Tarcher, 1989.

Gardner, Howard. *Frames of Mind*. N.p.: Basic Books, 1993.

Gelb, Michael J. *How to Think Like Leonardo da Vinci*. New York: Delacorte Press, 1998.

Gross, Ron. *Peak Learning*. New York: Jeremy P. Tarcher, 1991.

Horn, Sam. *Concentration!* Menlo Park, CA: Crisp Publications, 1991.

Lengefeld, Uelaine. *Study Skills Strategies*. Menlo Park, CA: Crisp Publications, 1994.

Loftus, Elizabeth. *Memory*. New York: Ardsley House Publishers, 1980.

Lorayne, Harry and Jerry Lucas. *The Memory Book*. New York: Ballantine Books, 1996.

Pauk, Walter. *How to Study in College, 6th Ed*. Boston: Houghton Mifflin, 1993.

Rose, Colin. *Accelerated Learning*. New York: Dell Books, 1989.

Siebert, Al. *The Adult Students Guide to Survival and Success*. N.p.: Practical Psychology Press, 1997.

Timm, Paul R. *Successful Self-Management*. Menlo Park, CA: Crisp Publications, 1987.

Wujec, Tom. *Pumping Ions*. New York: Doubleday, 1998.

# Now Available From

## Books•Videos•CD-ROMs•Computer-Based Training Products

## Subject Areas Include:

*Management*

*Human Resources*

*Communication Skills*

*Personal Development*

*Marketing/Sales*

*Organizational Development*

*Customer Service/Quality*

*Computer Skills*

*Small Business and Entrepreneurship*

*Adult Literacy and Learning*

*Life Planning and Retirement*

# CRISP WORLDWIDE DISTRIBUTION

English language books are distributed worldwide. Major international distributors include:

## ASIA/PACIFIC

*Australia/New Zealand:* In Learning, PO Box 1051, Springwood QLD, Brisbane, Australia 4127   Tel: 61-7-3-841-2286, Facsimile: 61-7-3-841-1580
ATTN: Messrs. Richard/Robert Gordon

*Malaysia, Philippines, Singapore:* Epsys Pte Ltd., 540 Sims Ave #04-01, Sims Avenue Centre, 387603, Singapore   Tel: 65-747-1964, Facsimile: 65-747-0162 ATTN: Mr. Jack Chin

*Hong Kong/Mainland China:* Crisp Learning Solutions, 18/F Honest Motors Building 9-11 Leighton Rd., Causeway Bay, Hong Kong   Tel: 852-2915-7119,
Facsimile: 852-2865-2815 ATTN: Ms. Grace Lee

*Japan:* Phoenix Associates, Believe Mita Bldg., 8th Floor 3-43-16 Shiba, Minato-ku, Tokyo 105-0014, Japan   Tel: 81-3-5427-6231,  Facsimile: 81-3-5427-6232
ATTN: Mr. Peter Owans

## CANADA

Crisp Learning Canada, 60 Briarwood Avenue, Mississauga, ON L5G 3N6 Canada
Tel: 905-274-5678, Facsimile: 905-278-2801
ATTN: Mr. Steve Connolly

## EUROPEAN UNION

*England:* Flex Learning Media, Ltd., 9-15 Hitchin Street,
Baldock, Hertfordshire, SG7 6AL, England
Tel: 44-1-46-289-6000, Facsimile: 44-1-46-289-2417   ATTN: Mr. David Willetts

## INDIA

Multi-Media HRD, Pvt. Ltd., National House, Floor 1
6 Tulloch Road, Appolo Bunder, Bombay, India 400-039
Tel: 91-22-204-2281, Facsimile: 91-22-283-6478
ATTN: Messrs. Ajay Aggarwal/ C.L. Aggarwal

## SOUTH AMERICA

*Mexico:* Grupo Editorial Iberoamerica, Nebraska 199, Col. Napoles, 03810 Mexico, D.F.
Tel: 525-523-0994, Facsimile: 525-543-1173   ATTN: Señor Nicholas Grepe

## SOUTH AFRICA

*Bookstores*: Alternative Books, PO Box 1345, Ferndale 2160, South Africa
Tel: 27-11-792-7730, Facsimile: 27-11-792-7787   ATTN: Mr. Vernon de Haas

*Corporate*: Learning Resources, P.O. Box 2806, Parklands, Johannesburg 2121, South Africa, Tel: 27-21-531-2923, Facsimile: 27-21-531-2944 ATTN: Mr. Ricky Robinson

## MIDDLE EAST

Edutech Middle East, L.L.C., PO Box 52334, Dubai U.A.E.
Tel: 971-4-359-1222, Facsimile: 971-4-359-6500   ATTN: Mr. A.S.F. Karim